BECOMING
—AN—
AUTISM
SUCCESS STORY

ANITA LESKO BSN, RN, MS, CRNA

ADVANCE PRAISE FOR
BECOMING AN AUTISM SUCCESS STORY

"Within a few years of getting diagnosed with autism at age fifty, Anita Lesko has arrived on the international stage for folks with autism. This outstanding book combines Lesko's hard-won insights, life strategies, direct guidance, science, and encouragement. This book is the antidote to 'can't'—Anita Lesko has defeated the naysayers and generously provides the path for others who struggle. While she visualizes herself as an advocate for people with autism, I can see her as an advocate for anyone who sets a lofty goal. (Don't hold back, Anita!)"

— Rachel Bédard, PhD, Licensed Psychologist, co-author of *Raising a Child on the Autism Spectrum* and *You've Got This: The Journey from Middle School to College*

"Anita Lesko is a poster child for someone with the gifts of autism! Her goal-oriented, positive attitude, intelligence, and laser-focused approach to any project guarantee positive results. She is eminently qualified to write this book and speak as an authority for those succeeding at 'thriving with autism!'"

— Craig Evans, Founder of Autism Hangout, co-author of *Been There. Done That. Try This!* and *Ask Dr. Tony!*

"The beautiful, descriptive words of this book will serve to inspire others, which is Anita Lesko's mission and purpose. She shares with honest vulnerability about her life experiences and gives practical solutions, not just for how to cope, but for how to thrive as a person with autism."

— Carol Vickers, M.A., PCC, Professional Coach and Facilitator

BECOMING AN AUTISM SUCCESS STORY

All marketing and publishing rights guaranteed to and reserved by:

FUTURE HORIZONS INC.

721 W. Abram Street
Arlington, TX 76013
(800) 489-0727
(817) 277-0727
(817) 277-2270 (fax)
E-mail: info@fhautism.com
www.fhautism.com

© 2019 Anita Lesko

Cover & interior design by John Yacio III

All rights reserved.
Printed in the USA.

ISBN: 9781941765975

I dedicate this book to my mom, Rita, for teaching me the power of the mind all those years ago, which enabled me to be where I am today. Also to my husband and soul mate, Abraham, for all his love and support. And to all on the autism spectrum, I dedicate myself to help enable you to unlock the power of your mind to achieve your dreams.

— ANITA LESKO

"The biggest adventure you can take
is to live the life of your dreams."

— OPRAH WINFREY

CONTENTS

CONTENTS

SPECIAL NOTE FROM TEMPLE GRANDIN

Both Anita Lesko and I are people on the autism spectrum who have successful careers. Anita is a highly successful nurse anesthetist who administers anesthesia to patients during brain surgeries and complex joint replacements. I am a professor of animal science at Colorado State University. Although our childhoods were much different, our paths to a good career are very similar.

Both of us learned the value of hard work at a young age. Anita earned horse riding lessons in exchange for cleaning the stables. Paying for riding lessons was beyond her financial means. Horses and riding were an important part of my teenage years, too. Anita was determined to learn to show horses and to, one day, jump them in competitions. She accomplished this while working her way up and earning privileges by cleaning the stalls. I was a poor student who had little interest in academics, so my school put me to work cleaning the stable and taking care of the horses. When I was ready to become interested in academics, my science teacher, Mr. Carlock, gave me interesting projects. It was then that academics became the path to my goal of becoming a scientist.

The next step for Anita was getting a job at an ice arena at the concession stand. She was eager to learn more interesting jobs such as running the spot lights and driving the Zamboni. She always wanted to try something new.

Both Anita and I did journalism. There is a scene in the HBO movie *Temple Grandin* where I go up to the editor of the Arizona Farmer Ranchman magazine and get the editor's card. I recognized that writing for the magazine would open many doors in the cattle industry. Anita started writing for aviation magazines and landed a ride in an F-15 fighter jet.

Determination and hard work enabled Anita to become the success she is today.

FOREWORD

Anita is a source of inspiration and information. Her description of the value of visualization and neuroplasticity will be of benefit to those of any age who have autism, as well as their family members, teachers, and therapists.

We have known for some time that those who have autism tend to learn by visualization and demonstration. The learning style also includes a propensity to seek patterns and to benefit from repetition. However, there can be a mind-body dissociation, delay in processing time, and a tendency to be distracted by social and sensory experiences. Anita discovered a way to visualize what she wanted her body to do, and by mentally rehearsing the actions in quiet solitude, she was able to "download" how to achieve complex abilities, thus effectively "rewiring" her brain. The procedure commences by first imagining the ability from her own visual perspective, then from the perspective of a spectator. Thus, her imagination initiates the neural pathways to bridge the mind/body division. When she then needs to demonstrate the ability, she is able to conceptualize, organize, and perform the actions efficiently and confidently.

Anita's book is a bridge between our knowledge of the neurology of autism and the latest scientific theories of neuroplasticity. The methods she taught herself, leading her to success, need to be integrated into school curriculum, job coaching, and therapy to facilitate skills that have previously been so elusive for those who have autism.

— *Professor Tony Attwood*
Minds and Hearts Clinic
Brisbane, Australia

INTRODUCTION

Before you begin reading this book, I'd like to say that it isn't an autobiography. Instead, it's a book that I visualize will change the world for individuals with autism, and *anyone* who wishes to achieve their dreams by rewiring their brain for success. I use my life's story as the backdrop of the message I want to get out there. I see visualization and neuroplasticity as the new wave of the future for anyone wanting a better life, to reach a goal, or make their dreams come true. *New York Times* bestselling author/ University of Toronto Professor Dr. Norman Doidge discusses how neuroplasticity can change the brain in his book *The Brain's Way of Healing: Remarkable Discoveries and Recoveries from the Frontiers of Neuroplasticity.*

I have autism, diagnosed at age fifty. I think in pictures, yes, just like Dr. Temple Grandin. As a young child, I felt like a little lost soul in a world I didn't understand. I was a total social misfit, I couldn't look anyone in the eye, and simply didn't know how to function. I was so uncoordinated that I tripped over my own feet. At the writing of this book, I just turned fifty-nine. I've been working for the past thirty years as a certified registered nurse anesthetist. I graduated from Columbia University in 1988 with my master's in nurse anesthesia. I've accomplished many things in my life thus far. I was a guest speaker at the United Nations Headquarters for World Autism Awareness Day 2017. I'm an author, national speaker, and a blogger. I'm also an internationally published military aviation photojournalist, and I've gotten to fly in an F-15 fighter jet and a Navy helicopter. In my younger days, I jumped horses over six-foot-high fences.

So, you wonder, how did this uncoordinated misfit kid do all of this? Well, I developed a passion. Then I figured out a way to visualize what I wanted my body to do. Eventually, my brain got re-wired to do the things I wanted it to—and then I did them. I would spend *hours* watching what I wanted to learn. During this long watching process, the steps would be downloading into my mind. Once recorded into my brain, I could play it back and watch it over and over with mental imagery to learn the skill. Here are several examples which are discussed later in the book. When I wanted to learn to ride, I spent hours watching beginners learning to ride, as well as advanced riding like jumping. I watched for many hours before actually getting on a horse. In my first riding lesson, I got to *feel* the sensations of the horses' movement. Then I was able to use my mental imagery by combining what I was visualizing with the actual sensations.

When I talk about this with my friend Temple, she discussed using this same method when she started out in her world-famous career with livestock. She spent hours watching the cattle getting vaccinated and how the handlers operated the vaccine device. After rehearsing that in her mind many times, one day she just picked up the vaccination gun and started vaccinating the cattle. Once she felt how to actually squeeze the handles on the device, it was downloaded permanently into her brain. She discusses this (and much more) in detail in her book *Thinking in Pictures*. I used these same methods to gain the social skills I greatly lacked. I watched people for *years* and took note of their facial expressions, how they look into each other's eyes while talking, how they move their body, etc. Once I started implementing these skills in my daily life, it became easier to initiate a conversation with someone and look them in the eye. I learned everything through long periods of watching others do these things. The more complex the activity, the longer I'd have to spend watching. I had endless obstacles to overcome, but I never gave up. Each and every obstacle became another possibility. Henry Ford has a great quote, "Obstacles are those frightful things you see when you take your eyes off your goal." I first heard that quote from my friend Dr. Temple Grandin about a year ago. When I heard it, I realized I've been living my whole life by this very quote. I forged ahead and figured out ways to accomplish goals. I developed techniques to visualize things, from how to ride a horse, figure skate, look people in the eye, socialize with others, work as an anesthetist, everything.

In the autism world, I see this as pioneering into a whole new frontier. However, it wasn't *just* the visualization, it was also my involvement with horses (my special interest) and all the childhood jobs I did. All my time spent with the horses served as what we now know as horse therapy, or "hippotherapy." I also worked many jobs in my late teens and early twenties which served to get me out in the world, socializing and interacting with others. I was a volunteer at a local hospital while I was in college, which opened the door to what evolved into my now thirty-year career. Altogether, I rewired my brain, enabling me to become totally functional in life and have a successful career. I believe that many others on the autism spectrum, as well as anyone, can also learn to use visualization to rewire their brains. This is known as *neuroplasticity*.

HIPPOTHERAPY + LIFE EXPERIENCE & SOCIALIZATION + VISUALIZATION & NEUROPLASTICITY = REWIRED BRAIN

Within the pages of this book, I'm going to discuss numerous things. It may seem like many different topics, yet they all fit together to create the whole picture: hippotherapy, life experience and socialization, visualization, neuroplasticity, rewiring the brain, the human-animal connection, and having a successful life.

Neuroplasticity has become a buzzword in psychology and scientific circles, and even outside of these arenas. There are promises that you can rewire your brain, enabling you to improve your life. Just following my passion for horses and dream to ride them awakened my brain to create new pathways for me to achieve my goals and enabled me to have a happy and fulfilling life. The changes in my brain's wiring stayed with me even after dismounting a horse. Before I started riding, I was trapped inside the prison of my autism, bound with invisible chains. I freed myself, yet didn't know I was using a scientific method now proven by evidence-based research. I was just a young girl who loved the power and majesty of horses and my deep connection with them. As I have come to learn, there are people such as neuroscientist Dr. Michael Merzenich who collaborated in numerous studies researching brain plasticity. For nearly five decades, he has been a leading pioneer in brain plasticity research. Dr. Merzenich has published more than 150 articles in leading peer-reviewed journals. He has received numerous awards and prizes including the Thomas Alva Edison Patent Award and one of the world's top neuroscience prizes, the Kavli Prize, for his achievements in the field of brain plasticity. My story is proof that all his research and writings are correct. Dr. Doidge has another NYT Bestselling book, *The Brain That Changes Itself*, with many excellent reviews; one of which is by the late Dr. Oliver Sacks, world-renowned neurologist, bestselling author and professor at NYU School of Medicine: "Fascinating. Doidge's book is a remarkable and hopeful portrait of the endless adaptability of the human brain." Dr. Sacks has been quoted saying he believed that the brain is the "most incredible thing in the universe."

INTRODUCTION

There are different ways of rewiring the brain through neuroplasticity. Karen Onderko, Research and Education Director at Integrated Learning Systems, states, "What stimulates neuroplasticity? The neurons (nerve calls) connect or reconnect and change the brain's structure and function when they are stimulated through repeated input. That input can be physical, sensory, or mental, depending on what we are trying to learn."[I] Throughout my life, I have been using a combination of all three.

In an article by Adrienne Warber, she mentioned, "When Dr. Norman Doidge was interviewed by CNN about a woman named Michelle Mack, who exhibited symptoms [of autism] such as behavioral and communication problems. A brain scan revealed the 95 percent of the left hemisphere of her brain was dead due to an in-utero stroke and that her right hemisphere had taken over functions normally handled by the left, such as speaking and reading. She has a savant talent for numbers and date recall. Dr. Doidge stated, 'that Mack's recovery was an example of the brain's ability to rewire or heal itself to compensate for injury.'"[II] An article in *The Guardian* states that "Doidge is careful to stress that the science behind neuroplasticity is still in the unformed state, and that just because the methods work for some people, they won't work for everyone."[III] Later in the book, neuroplasticity and visualization will be covered in detail.

This book will change the way you look at autism and the power of the mind. I will always be on the autism spectrum. I will never be a neurotypical person. But I've rewired my brain in ways that enabled me to function at full capacity at a high-stress job, develop exceptional executive functioning, social skills, the ability to develop a relationship and get married, run a household, and function in everyday life. I have achieved what every parent of a child on the spectrum dreams of, for their child to be fully independent after they're gone. I can help others on the autism spectrum achieve the same results. But it's not just for those on the spectrum, it's for *anyone* who has a dream or goal they hope to reach.

I have a dream of totally changing the world's view of autism. I am visualizing that this book will open the door for those on the autism spectrum to step through to their new lives. Once people begin learning to use visualization to rewire their brains, neuroplasticity will ignite this process. Occasionally, someone will ask me if I wish I didn't have autism. Not a chance. I wouldn't have experienced all the exciting things I've done thus far, and I wouldn't be at a point in my life that I inspire others and change lives. That is the greatest gift of all.

— **Anita Lesko**

CHAPTER 1

LEARNING A POWERFUL LESSON FOR LIFE

"When you want to do something bad enough, you have the power within you to make it happen."

— RITA LESKO

CHAPTER 1

Many years ago, I was a little lost soul in a world I didn't understand. At home I always felt a sense of peace, comfort, and security. The only person I felt comfortable with was my mom; she was the only one I would speak to when I started talking at two. The moment I stepped out the door, I instantly felt massive anxiety. I didn't understand people: their words, body language, or how I was supposed to react to any of it. Perhaps you can imagine if you were dropped off in a foreign country and didn't speak or understand the language. You would have no clue what anyone was talking about or how you would fit in and make them understand what your thoughts or needs were. It was not only frightening, but it enveloped me with a deep sadness and loss of self-worth. I recognized at a very early age that I was different than others. My mom told me that at age four I asked her why other children didn't want to be my friend, and why they all seemed so different than me.

A LIFE-CHANGING EVENT

I had a life-changing moment when I discovered, at the age of fifty, that I'm on the autism spectrum. Until then I had never heard of Asperger's syndrome or known anyone with autism. I realized I was different, never fit in, and that I had seemingly unusual sensory and social issues, but I thought I was the only person in the world like this. One night at work, a co-worker entered the lounge where I was sitting. She was crying and gushing that her son has just been diagnosed with Asperger's syndrome. Furrowing my brows, I asked her what Asperger's was. She was holding some papers in her hand which she then extended toward me. I looked down and started reading and my eyes grew wider by the second. The top line read,

"If you have ten out of twelve of these symptoms, you have Asperger's syndrome." I was numb by the time I reached number twelve. I had *all* the symptoms. It was that moment that the pieces of the puzzle of my life fell into place. There were the answers to all the questions I'd been asking for the past fifty years. I have Asperger's syndrome! That night after work, I stopped at the bookstore and got every book they had about Asperger's and stayed up all night reading. Three weeks later, I went for a formal diagnosis by a neuropsychologist.

In addition to reading all the books I got about Asperger's, I was feverishly researching online. I quickly discovered Asperger's was on the autism spectrum, typically referred to as being on the "high end" of this spectrum. The current *Diagnostic and Statistical Manual of Mental Disorders, 5th Edition: DSM-5* classifies Asperger's as simply being under the umbrella of autism. As my research continued, the name "Temple Grandin" kept appearing, so I began reading about her. The first video that I saw of Temple was a documentary: *The Woman Who Thinks Like a Cow*. I immediately identified with this fascinating woman. The more she talked about cows and how they think and react to their environment, the more excited I became. That was exactly how I was with horses! Years later, Temple and I would become good friends, and I would write a book about her, *Temple Grandin: The Stories I Tell My Friends*. Life is always full of surprises!

As I would realize later in life, it would be horses that broke the barrier between my autism and the world. Horses were the key that opened the door to enable me to earn my master's degree from Columbia University in nurse anesthesia and have my now thirty-year career as a certified registered nurse anesthetist. Horses also empowered me to shatter my social barriers, which not only served to help in my career, but ultimately enabled me to have a relationship that turned into love and marriage with my husband (who is also on the autism spectrum). I have become a very strong autism activist and had the distinct honor of speaking at the United Nations Headquarters in New York City for World Autism Awareness Day 2017.

There were several other key components that worked together to put all the pieces together: neuroplasticity, visualization, and working many different jobs in my late teens and early twenties to obtain life experience and practice socialization. With all these tools combined, I rewired my brain in the most positive way possible to become an autism success story.

THE UNCOORDINATED MISFIT KID

When I was a child, I recognized I was different from others because I had severe problems with coordination—my body simply had no perception of my arms and legs or what they were doing. I would describe it as having no signals sent from my limbs to my brain (and vice-versa) in reaction to my environment. I was always tripping, falling, dropping things, and simply looking awkward. It was most apparent when I started kindergarten. All the other children seemed to effortlessly run, play, and do physical activities without any struggles. I'd watch every move they all made, recognizing I was very different than they were, simply on coordination alone. I couldn't understand why my body wouldn't cooperate with me. Try as I might, it just wasn't happening. Despite my early age, I would watch the other kids moving freely and happily and feel very sad inside that I couldn't be like them. Of course, my sloppy, uncoordinated gait and movements were fodder for every bully in the land.

To this day, I have an unusual gait. I walk in a very distinct way. It's not very feminine; I look more like I'm trudging through mud with muck boots on. As I walk, my right arm stays stationary at my side, yet my left arm swings back and forth freely. This was all more pronounced when I was young. When I'd trip, I felt as if there were no connection between my feet and my brain. My body couldn't react fast enough to thrust out my arms to break the fall. Thus, I'd be going face-first into the ground. After the fact, I'd be on the ground wondering how it happened. When I fell on the playground at school during recess, some of the boys would run over to kick me. It wasn't bad enough simply to fall, I was literally kicked when I was down.

As I progressed to second, third, and fourth grade, the stakes got higher in the physical education classes. They wanted us to play team games. Back in the day, team selection was made by the students themselves, so as the class misfit I always was the last one standing with neither team wanting me on their side. That really dragged my morale and psyche down the drain. Of course, a person will have little to no self-esteem when things like this consistently occur. Whichever team I ended up on, the disappointed looks on everyone's faces said it all. Fortunately, from all I read and hear, in schools today teams aren't picked in that manner just for that reason.

While I was obviously not gifted in sports, I loved to do arts and crafts with my mom. We'd sit for hours by the dining room table with all sorts of fun things like colored construction paper, glitter, glue, fabrics, fuzzy pipe cleaners, and my least favorite thing: scissors. It took quite a long time to master those darn things. Mom would show me again and again, but it just made no sense to me. One day she got up, stood behind my chair, and instructed me to pick up the scissors. Once they were in my hand, she put her hand over mine as if she were going to use them and helped me open and close the scissors until I was doing it well on my own. Then, she picked up a sheet of red construction paper and gave it to me to hold in my left hand. I was able to cut the paper successfully! Once I mastered that, she would have me cut out shapes; simple ones at first, then more complex. Eventually, I graduated to making intricate snowflakes from white paper folded in half.

Scissors were one thing. Walking and everyday activities were another. Any kind of physical activity was unpleasant for me. Because I felt no perception of what my body was doing, I was constantly getting hurt. Fortunately, I have always had a very high pain tolerance. As I mentioned earlier, I was so slow to react to falling, if at all, that I'd always end up flat on my face. Once I was attempting to play on a neighbor's dolly they had out on their driveway. Their kids were stepping on it like it was a skateboard and gliding effortlessly across the driveway. I had been watching them for quite some time thinking how fun it looked, so I went over there and asked if I could try it. They instructed me to put one foot on the dolly and push on the driveway with the other foot. I did exactly what they said and the next thing I knew I was flying forward, the dolly flipped out from under me, and landing face first onto the concrete driveway. I remember the stinging pain on my face and looking down at a lot of blood. The kids were laughing at me. I got up and ran home, managing not to erupt into tears until inside. My upper lip was bleeding and my upper front tooth was chipped off at the gum line.

DIFFICULTY FOLLOWING ALONG
WITH MOVEMENTS

Sometimes at school during gym class, the teacher had everyone stand facing her to follow along with a series of exercises. She would first demonstrate what she wanted us to do, then all the students would follow along. Everyone, that is, except me. I would attempt to follow the exact movements, but my eyes didn't seem to relay the message fast enough to my brain, or my brain didn't send the message fast enough to my body for it to respond. It resulted in me looking like a fool, desperately trying to follow along with all my heart, only to fail, become totally frustrated, and begin to cry. No matter how slowly the teacher demonstrated the movements, I simply couldn't process the input to replicate the movements. It would feel as if my brain shut down, like it just froze up and couldn't function. At that point, nothing was going to get me to be able to follow along. I still can't follow things like a dance routine, for example, unless I spend a good amount of time visualizing it by breaking it down into pieces first.

Back in the 90s, a song and dance routine called "the Macarena" became all the rage. Everyone was doing it. It was a pretty catchy tune, and I wanted to do it, too. I'd try to follow along with others without any luck; it had too many movements in too fast a succession. I desperately wanted to do this silly routine! So, I visualized it from start to finish, *very* slowly, step by step, and broke the dance down into many pieces. It took over a week for my brain to process it, but finally I was able to do it from start to finish. I was so thrilled! I would wonder for years as to why others could simply do it on the first attempt. I would watch dancers learning new routines and pick it up immediately. I was fascinated, yet baffled.

8

CHAPTER 1

As I would learn later, I would have to mentally review movements in my head for at least a week, visualizing the movements over and over before I could replicate the particular activity. I realized this once I began to ride horses, when I couldn't respond to the instructor's request to do something during the lesson. I found that, despite being unable to perform in that moment, I could do so later after replaying the motions in my mind dozens of times. This was extremely baffling and annoying to some of the riding instructors I had over the years. Some took it in stride, while others would yell at me. I was trying, but when your mind and body aren't "connected" it can make things rather difficult. I would typically tell the riding instructor that I would be able to perform the action the following week, after I could spend quiet time visualizing it multiple times. They would look at me like I was crazy. "Why can't you just do it now like I'm telling you?" they would ask. My reply was always the same: "I don't know. I just know that I have to visualize myself doing it over and over and over, like I'm programming it into my head. Next week I will be able to do it." And sure enough, the next week in the next lesson I could demonstrate the skill. At first, I thought everyone else learned like that. I quickly found out they don't, that others could instantly respond to what the instructor told them to do. The positive thing is that I discovered I did have the ability to learn, just in a different way. That was just one of many gifts horseback riding gave to me.

MY CONNECTION TO ANIMALS

I also realized at an early age that I had a very special connection to animals. Any animal that I encountered wanted to be my friend; they instantly took to me like bees to honey. Animals accepted me for who I was. That brought a special joy to my heart, bringing that sense of peace, comfort, and security that I only felt at home with my mom. I eventually became fascinated with studying the behaviors of horses in particular. I recognized that I could easily figure out what they were thinking and how they would respond to their environment. I felt a deep connection to them. They seemed to experience the world around them very much like myself, thus explaining the bond I felt for these majestic animals. This bond is so significant it is recognized worldwide in many areas. The American Veterinary Medical Association states, "The human-animal bond is a mutually beneficial and dynamic relationship between people and animals that is influenced by behaviors essential to the health and wellbeing of both. This includes, among other things, emotional, psychological, and physical interactions of people, animals, and the environment."[IV]

Horses seemed to be extremely sensitive to their environments, just as I was. Because I didn't discover I'm on the autism spectrum until I was fifty, all those years I had no idea why I was different and never fit in. What I did know was that every animal accepted me. They gave me great solace. This is not and was not limited to horses, but cats, dogs, bunnies, birds, and even raccoons.

THE HUMAN-ANIMAL CONNECTION

For many people, having an animal in their life is very important. It doesn't matter what kind of animal it is, having a furry friend is a source of joy. For some, it's far beyond that. Specifically, for an individual on the autism spectrum, an animal companion could make all the difference in the world to them. I have included many sources of research findings throughout this book. I like to validate things to verify their truth and significance. This is no different.

During my research to gather information for this book, I found many exciting things. Writing a book is a journey and I learned a lot along the way. I found some great videos about this topic. Here is a quote by the filmmaker Dennis Zaidi: "Millions of people are affected by circumstances where the human-animal connection could help, yet they remain uninformed of its potential. Thousands of organizations remain underfunded and underutilized for the simple reason that the general public is unaware they even exist." This is very true.

I am amazed and thrilled to see all the different kinds of research projects directed at the human-animal connection. At Tufts University/Tufts Institute for Human-Animal Interaction, many studies are currently underway. One is about animal-assisted interventions and anxiety reduction. Emerging evidence suggests animal contact might be used to reduce anxiety, but little is known about which specific aspects of human-animal interaction produce therapeutic effects.

Investigations are being conducted to look at animal-assisted interventions for child literacy, youth development, and the human-animal interaction and veterinary medicine, to name a few. The list goes on and on. As you see, there is much to be gained in our lives with the involvement of animals in it. I'm not a researcher, but I can testify that animals enrich your life and often can help to empower you, as was my experience with horses.

I found an article from the *New York Times* which talks about pet ownership and how much it has climbed in the past few years. The article, dated 2011, states that about two-thirds of American households include at least one pet. Here's what it said: "Checking the latest stats, 68 percent of U.S. households—about 85 million families—own a pet, according to the 2017-2018 National Pet Owners Survey conducted by the American Pet Products Association. In 1988, for comparison, only 56 percent of U.S. households had a pet. People are passionate about their companion animals … In studies done on why people refused to evacuate New Orleans during Hurricane Katrina, a surprising number said they could not leave their pets behind."[v]

I can tell you that I relate to all of these tidbits of information. I live in Pensacola, Florida and I was here during Hurricane Ivan, a category four hurricane, when it made landfall just to the west of Pensacola. That put my area in the upper right quadrant, the most intense part of a hurricane. At that time, I had ten cats and three horses, my house was surrounded by 100-foot-tall trees, and my elderly parents lived with me. I made the decision to get all of us out of the house and go to a hotel that I deemed would be safe during the storm. So, at five in the morning, with the hurricane taking direct aim at Pensacola, I put all the cats and my parents in the car and went to the hotel across town to check in. Of course, animals weren't allowed. No problem. I requested a room at the far end of the building by the back exit door. After checking in, I went back to the car and basically sat in the vehicle with all the cats in their carriers and the air conditioner running until darkness began to set in, which was early due to the impending storm. I had already taken my parents in the room and they were resting. One carrier at a time, I snuck them in through the back door. I first covered each carrier with a jacket, so it wasn't so obvious. It took a while, but finally I had all the carriers inside our hotel room. The cats sensed something was very wrong. I could see the petrified looks on their faces. The barometric pressure was rapidly dropping, and I, too, could feel the difference in the atmosphere. They were all as quiet

CHAPTER 1

as a church mouse. Not one of them made a peep. I gave them all food and water in their carriers; I didn't want to let them out in case the windows got broken by flying debris. As the night set in, so did the howling winds. The electricity went out at eleven at night. As the wee hours closed in, the force of the wind made the building sway. We were all huddled in the bathroom. I had stacked up all the carriers in the bathtub. The water in the toilet was sloshing back and forth, even splashing over the seat from the violent winds outside. We all sat in silence, looking at each other by the light of the battery-operated lantern, listening to the sounds of the raging hurricane. Suddenly, the fire alarms started going off and the water sprinkling system started spraying water everywhere. Then came the pounding on our door by a man yelling to get out of the room and get to the front foyer of the hotel, that the roof had ripped off the entire building and people were swept away. As I write this, I can very clearly remember the feeling of mass hysteria inside my whole body. I was convinced we were all going to die. Winds were over 140 mph with gusts over 180 mph. Moments before the fire alarm had gone off, there was a massive sound like a freight train coming through the building. It was a tornado. That's what took the roof off the four-story hotel, and as we'd see in the morning at dawn, it tore off the entire stairwell right outside the exit door—just feet away from our room. When we were ordered to evacuate the room, I looked at my mom and said, "These cats are all coming with us. I'm not leaving them in here." So out we ran, with all the carriers, into the darkness of the long hallway, illuminated only by the light of others with flashlights or battery lanterns. I gasped at what I saw. One after another, doors flung open and people emerged with all kinds of animals. No one said a word. It was eerie to see all of this unfolding in the shadows. Cats, dogs, a huge great Dane, two peacocks, a miniature pig, puppies, kittens, children crying, adults crying, and my parents, five cat carriers, and I all filed into the hallway. Water was still spewing from the sprinklers on the ceiling and pouring down from around every light fixture. Because the roof had been ripped off, the rain was coming directly into the building. Everyone and their animals were saturated. I sat on the floor, literally paralyzed with fear. You could see and hear the walls and ceiling swaying. Any second, they might come down. Not one animal made a sound; I was amazed by that. Between the animals and the overflow of water, it was like Noah's ark had come to life. It was around two-thirty in the morning when the last working radio stated that the eye of the hurricane just made landfall and the worst of it was past us. I burst out crying hysterically at that point, as did most others, men and women alike. Everyone stayed in the foyer until the faint hint of daybreak came. The conversation was all about the animals and how no one was going to leave them behind. We were all standing in six inches of water, but I had made sure to run back to a room to get chairs to put the carriers on. We were all safe, and so were our pets.

At dawn, I went outside to see the destruction. As I opened the door, the smell of pine trees and wood filled the air. My eyes nearly popped out when I saw the whole roof of the building shattered and the gaping hole that was once the top floor. The base of trees eight feet in diameter were snapped off like matchsticks; from the branches of the few trees that were still standing dangled everything from clothing, smaller trees, wires from electrical poles, and even the poles themselves. It was shocking. I felt numb, like a zombie. Mass destruction was everywhere you looked. Homes had been shattered with only the concrete slab left behind. It was something that is etched in my mind forever.

CHAPTER 1

My next fear was the horses. I was convinced they didn't make it through the hurricane. I had read hurricane safety for horses and it said to never put them in the barn and to leave them outside. I did as it directed and had locked the barn doors so they couldn't get inside the building. Hours later, when we made our way back home, I saw the whole barn was destroyed. It looked as if a bomb had blown it up. I couldn't see the horses anywhere and started calling out to them by their names. Suddenly, my big horse, Lars, neighed out at the top of his lungs. I started running toward the direction it came from. There they were, all three just fine, standing down in a ravine. Somehow, they instinctively knew to go to the lowest area to ride out the storm. When I saw them, I literally fell to the ground crying. All of my emotions just made me drop flat out, face down, crying and gasping for air. The house was half destroyed. Trees were down everywhere. It was mass destruction. But I was beyond happy that all my animals had survived it all.

That night during Ivan at that hotel, the human-animal bond was obvious, without any need for researchers or studies to confirm it. All those people smuggled their beloved pets into that hotel just like I did. It was a very profound experience.

THE PONY RIDE THAT WOULD
SET ME FREE

I encountered my first horse at the age of two. It was a small black pony at a pony ride concession in a nearby park. Little did I know on that fateful day that a lifelong journey would begin, ultimately enabling me to break free from the chains that held me trapped inside of myself. Each horse I ever met played a significant role in my escape to freedom and to living a happy, productive life.

BECOMING AN AUTISM SUCCESS STORY

I can still remember looking at the pony's eyes and feeling a very tranquil peace deep within me. The fur, the mane, and the squeaky sound the saddle made when I sat on it all made me happy. The movement when the pony started to walk was magical. It sent a shock wave of excitement throughout my entire body. It was extremely difficult for them to remove me from that pony, as I simply refused to let go of the saddle and had a meltdown until they would start leading the pony around the track again. Even if there were no spare quarters, I wanted to go to the track just to look at all the ponies.

I felt a deep connection to horses from that point on. They seemed to experience the world around them very much like myself, thus explaining the bond I felt for these majestic animals. Horses are extremely sensitive to many things, and they react accordingly. I had those same sensitivities, which I felt no one else appeared to have.

When I was around horses, I felt different. I felt like the person I wished I could really be: free, capable of doing anything, empowered, far from all emotional pain. I became obsessed with horses and everything about them. The saddle was my sanctuary. It awakened all my senses, enabling me to experience the world around me on a very different level. I didn't know I was on the autism spectrum, or how that affects literally every aspect of your life, from sensory issues, social challenges, learning difficulties, inability to make or keep friends, physical clumsiness and low self-esteem, to the struggles faced each day. I went through my first fifty years thinking I was all alone. Little did I know there are millions of others on the autism spectrum. The latest information released from the Centers for Disease Control (CDC) in Atlanta, Georgia is that about 1.7 percent—or 1 in 59—children are identified with autism spectrum disorder.[VI] This is quite an increase from one in sixty-eight.

THE MOST IMPORTANT ADVICE EVER: A STORY ABOUT COAL

When I was a little girl, our house was heated by an antiquated coal furnace down in our basement next to a huge coal bin. In the early fall, a big truck would come and back down our steep driveway. They would open a little window above the coal bin and insert a metal chute, which came from the truck laden with tons of coal. Once the chute was properly secured, the back of the truck would raise up and the coal would roar down the metal chute into the bin in our basement.

I was fascinated. The coal was comprised of shiny jet-black stones, each one misshapen and ranging from one to two inches in size. It made such a deafening sound as those chunks were racing down the chute that I had to squeeze my hands tightly over my ears to decrease the noise. Mom would always be standing there holding my hand tightly to be sure I didn't get too close to danger.

Once all the coal was unloaded into the bin, I would excitedly spend hours feeling the pieces of coal, examining each one to marvel at the intricacies of each piece. Like snowflakes, each one was different. We were the only ones in the neighborhood who had our house heated by coal, which attracted neighbors to come and watch the coal being delivered. It wasn't until I was older that I understood we had coal because we were poor.

It wasn't easy to get a fire going or to keep it going in the coal furnace. I'd watch my mom and dad getting it ready to start the fire. It was quite an art. Then, there were the endless trips down to the basement to keep adding just the right amount of coal to keep the fire going during the day and night in the winter. It was like a full-time job.

One winter, when I was six years old, will stand out in my

mind forever. Mom had a bad heart and lungs because she had rheumatic fever when she was thirteen. It had been below freezing for days and she had developed a bad case of pneumonia, diagnosed at the hospital after an elderly neighbor had taken us to the emergency room (my dad was at work, and we only had the one car). The doctor wanted to admit her to the hospital, but she refused because there was no one to take care of me. They sent her home with antibiotics instead. I can remember being really scared because I could see just how sick my mom was. She had a raging fever and was incredibly weak. I was terrified she was going to die.

As soon as we returned home, she somehow made her way upstairs to get in bed. Several hours later, the house started getting very cold, so cold you could see your breath. The coal furnace had gone out because no one had been adding coal to the fire.

Mom got up to go down to the basement to start a new fire. I watched her, ever so slowly, make her way down two flights of stairs. She was terribly out of breath from the pneumonia and was coughing up nasty chunks of phlegm tinged with blood from her lungs. She stopped at each step, gasping a few breaths, then slowly kept going to the next step.

Once down by the furnace, she began the process of building a new fire, using small kindling and pieces of coal carefully arranged into a pyramid. After there was a strong fire going, she added more coal and silently began the journey back upstairs.

I quietly trailed her back up there. She got herself over to the couch and literally collapsed onto it. I covered her with several blankets; her teeth were chattering from chills. I sat down on a chair next to the couch. I was scared and didn't know what else to do. Finally, after what seemed an eternity, I watched her fall asleep. I didn't leave her side. What I didn't understand was how she did all she had done, considering how deathly ill she was.

She only slept for about half an hour. When she opened her eyes, she saw me sitting there exactly as I had been before she fell asleep. With tears in my eyes, I asked, "How were you able to do all that when you are so sick?"

With her wise look, she replied: "The power of the mind." I looked puzzled. She knew I had no clue what she meant, so she continued, "I want you to always remember this day. I want you to remember that your mind is extremely powerful. You can will yourself to do things that might otherwise seem impossible. If you want to do something bad enough, and you keep telling yourself that you can do it, your mind will enable you to do whatever it is you want to do. Do you remember when I told you how I had rheumatic fever when I was a young girl?"

I did recall that story. I nodded yes.

"I was bed-ridden for four years. Isolated from the world. Parents wouldn't let their kids come to visit me because they were scared I was contagious. The only person who ever came to see me was a teacher from my school. She came each week and would bring a stack of books for me to read. She knew I loved learning about other countries, so many of the books were about far-away places. I would read each one and travel there in my mind. I would create images in extreme detail, so I could experience it as if I were really there. The sounds, smells, every sensation, I would feel. I would visualize it like a movie scene I was watching, and then as if I were actually there.

"That was when I discovered that your mind is extremely powerful. Today, yes, I'm terribly sick, but when the furnace went out I knew I had to go down there to start a new fire. It's going to be hours before your dad gets home from work. The pipes probably would freeze if I didn't do it, and I can't let us be cold. I willed my mind to enable me to have the strength to go downstairs to do it. When you want to do something bad enough, you have the power within you to make it happen."

I was listening to every word she said. I etched it permanently into my mind. I recognized this was big, something I would use throughout my life.

Mom sat up on the couch, still wrapped in the blankets. She took a deep breath and explained, "Let me give you an example of the power your mind can have on your whole body. You can be in a great mood. You are feeling happy: the sun is shining, the birds are singing, and you are outside enjoying the beautiful day. Suddenly, the phone rings, and it's someone calling you with really bad news.

"In an instant, after hearing the bad news, you feel sick all over, from head to toe. You feel nauseated, like you're going to faint, break out in a sweat, burst out crying. All of that happens in a second. You heard the bad news, and your mind causes all of that to happen. That is powerful.

"On the same token, you can use that same power of your mind to do positive things. It is all up to you. You must always remember this. You have the power within to accomplish what you have to do."

On that freezing winter day, now over fifty years ago, my mother gave me the wisdom and the insight into the power of the mind. I was only a young girl, yet I felt wise beyond my years. When I had goals I was desperate to achieve, I began visualizing what I needed to do, always remembering my mother's statement. You can use the power of your mind to visualize what you want to do, and do it.

CHAPTER 1

Only now in the twenty-first century have we learned how the mind can transform lives through this process. The brain's plasticity is a superpower for self-improvement. The world's most elite Olympic athletes use visualization to help them win gold medals. People are using it to change their lives in amazingly positive ways. You have within yourself the ability to change your brain through visualization, too.

CHAPTER 2

VISUALIZATION AND NEUROPLASTICITY

"I think in pictures. Words are like a second language to me. I translate both spoken and written words into full-color movies, complete with sound, which run like a VCR tape in my head."

– DR. TEMPLE GRANDIN

CHAPTER 2

I too, think in pictures. My whole life runs in my mind like a movie playing, and I can recall every last detail. I experience it as if I'm living an IMAX movie, but with all my senses active: touch, smell, sight, taste. Everything. It is as if the event is happening to me at that very moment. I always believed that everyone else thought like that, it never occurred to me that it could be any other way. I learned that everyone doesn't think like me when I first learned about Temple Grandin and read her books after being diagnosed. When Temple talked about being a visual thinker and explained it wasn't how everyone processed thought, I was pretty shocked!

I first "met" Temple back in 2011, just after getting diagnosed and writing a memoir: *Asperger's Syndrome: When Life Hands You Lemons, Make Lemonade*. Temple featured me in a book she was writing, *Different ... Not Less*. I am in chapter seven, "Nurse Anesthetist and Military Aviation Photographer" (which you'll learn more about later!). I met her in person in 2013 at an autism conference I had organized and we kept in contact over the years, periodically talking on the phone. In March of 2017, I decided to write a book about her to let the rest of the world get to know her as I did. While I was conducting the sixty hours of personal interviews with Temple, no matter what we talked about, she instantly recalled the event—even those from when she was a little kid—in explicit detail. You can read all the great stories Temple shared with me in *Temple Grandin: The Stories I Tell My Friends*.

I used visualization throughout my entire life to "program" my brain to do what I wanted it to. Temple does the same thing. In her HBO movie, *Temple Grandin*, they show how she uses visualization to test-run her cattle-handling facility in her mind.

I, somehow, figured out at a very early age that I needed to visualize myself doing something in order to be able to actually do it. The more complex the activity I was aiming for, the more frequently I needed to visualize it. I had to break everything down into individual pieces so I could focus on each step. Once I had each step ingrained in my mind, only then could I begin the slow process of putting it all together for the whole activity. I would visualize performing the task, focusing on every inch of my body, what it needed to do, and how it would feel. It typically took a full week to train myself to do something new. Here's the key: it had to be something I *wanted* to do. When I want to do something, I pull out all the stops! My perseverance is unwavering and I won't give up until I reach my goal, no matter how far-fetched or seemingly unrealistic it is to achieve. I will visualize my long-range goal frequently to keep up my motivation.

USING ALL YOUR SENSES

When I use visualization, I employ all my senses. I envision how it will feel, what I will hear, what I will see, etc. I visualize everything in my mind from start to finish. By the time I do the activity, it is as if I've done it a hundred times already. Often, I talk out loud to myself as I go over each step. Sometimes, I write it out in the same details I mentally broke it down into. I go through every little step of how I want it to turn out. I tend to do this with my eyes closed, actually feeling my entire body performing. I am in complete control of myself and my thoughts, including the ability to tune out any negative thoughts. It is imperative to maintain a positive focus. It's absolutely crucial to not allow your visualization to fail; for example, when visualizing jumping a horse over a huge course in competition, I do not even think for a moment of falling or having a wreck. If you do that, you would be actually training your muscles to fail. Once I visualize everything from start to finish, then I replay it repeatedly. I also learned that it's a good idea to visualize several scenarios in my mind in case I need an alternate route to accomplish the task.

VISUALIZING FROM TWO PERSPECTIVES

I visualize my goal from two different perspectives. I visualize myself, from head to toe, doing the activity from my own perspective. Once I have that embedded in my memory, I envision myself performing from the perspective of a spectator, as if I am watching a movie. Then I can see myself doing it perfectly. Once I'm at that point, I feel reassured and confident that I will be able to reproduce the activity. Over the years, all of this gave me a great sense of mental awareness, a heightened sense of well-being, and increased confidence in myself in the saddle. Eventually, that confidence allowed me to have better social interactions and to be more adept at doing activities other than those which were horse-related. Every visualization would be in movie-theater style, creating an overwhelming feeling to all my senses. I would be in a "zone" while conducting these sessions. In essence, my visual rehearsals were rewiring my mind so my body could actually perform the skill I was imagining.

SPORTS PSYCHOLOGY

I am fascinated by the field of sports psychology, which appears to keep growing based on all the research results which continue to accumulate. The majority of sports psychology practitioners utilize techniques similar to my visualization routine, including:

1. **Performance Enhancement** – This is where the athlete visualizes their performance in a positive way to trick their brain into thinking they have already done it. By using this mental imagery over and over, they are rewiring their brain, allowing them to excel at their sport. This is the most commonly utilized practice and it basically results in the athlete programming what their performance will be.

2. **Resilience and Injury Recovery** – This is what my mom taught me all those years ago as she willed herself down the stairs while sick. Using the power of the mind, athletes are trained to heal and be resilient after an injury or any setback.

3. **Motivation and Emotional Stress** – Anyone can get emotionally stressed and lack motivation. It is up to the sports psychologist to figure out what the underlying cause is and come up with a plan to get that athlete back on track and motivated.

PERFORMANCE ENHANCEMENT

One of my favorite Olympic athletes is Lindsey Vonn. In an article I found about visualization, it is reported that "one of the most successful female skiers in history, Lindsey Vonn, Olympic gold medalist says her mental practice gives her a competitive advantage on the course. 'I visualize the run before I do it. By the time I get to the starting gate, I've run that race 100 times already in my mind, picturing how I'll take the turns.' Vonn doesn't just keep the images in her head. She's also known to physically simulate the path by literally shifting her weight back and forth as if she were on skis, as well as practice the specific breathing patterns she'll use during the race. She says, 'I love that exercise. Once I visualize a course, I never forget it. So, I get on those lines and go through exactly the run I want to have.'" [VII]

CHAPTER 2

I believe that visualization is one of the most powerful means of achieving personal goals. First, you must have an idea or a dream. Then use the powers of visualization to get you there. Of course, one needs to realize that you must be willing to work extremely hard to achieve your dream. It doesn't simply happen because you visualize it!

Sports psychology can even help people off the playing field. The same strategies that sports psychologists use to teach athletes relaxation techniques, mental rehearsals, and cognitive restructuring are also useful in the workplace and everyday life. An individual on the autism spectrum can most definitely benefit from these same techniques. I am proof of that. Though I didn't know about sports psychology back then, I somehow instinctively knew what to do to enable myself to accomplish goals that would have been otherwise impossible.

I also now realize the extreme importance of physical activity for those on the autism spectrum in childhood and teen years as well as adulthood. I'm not talking about the physical activity one gets at school; those activities typically combine proprioceptive and spatial skills, which most people with autism lack. When we can't perform the activity like the neurotypical students, it leads to humiliation, decreased self-esteem, and more bullying. Meaningful physical activity must come from something you like to do and want to do. Exercise for those on the autism spectrum is critical for self-regulation and can also help them to process their environment. Unfortunately, an individual with autism may develop a negativity toward physical activity because of the experiences they had at school. That's why it is imperative to seek activities outside of school that are enjoyable and provide some form of exercise.

RESILIENCE AND RECOVERY INJURY

I learned early on that when I was going to ride, I needed to first go scope out the arena and look around for anything that might spook the horse. Also, even while in the saddle, to always be on the lookout for anything going on around the arena that was a potential threat to my safety. Any tiny little thing can send a horse into fear mode and react to it. Horses are animals of prey. Since the horse's principle means of survival in the wild has been his vigilance and speed, his flight reflex has been fine-tuned for millennia to be prepared to escape at the first suggestion of a threat. Horses who shy are often simply displaying a well-preserved flight reflex.[VIII]

For example, once I was schooling a young horse who was very green, and I don't mean the color. "Green," in this case, means inexperienced with little time under saddle. As I rode around the field, I didn't notice when a fellow rider took off her bright red winter coat and tossed it over the mounting block. In an instant, my horse spotted it and leaped up into the air, bucking as she landed and bolting away in the opposite direction. The initial leap unseated me enough that as she landed and took off, I was precariously hanging off the side of her. I saw galloping legs and her hooves flying. The ground appeared as if it were whizzing by. I was desperately trying to stay on, but another buck and her careening suddenly to the right was the final thing that catapulted me off and sent me smashing into a fence post, head first.

When I hit that fence post and the ground, I sustained five fractures and a concussion. I got up and very slowly made my way back to the house. It took about an hour and a half to accomplish that. I have a high pain tolerance, but all of that was a bit too much to handle. I refused to go to the hospital. I kept thinking I'd feel better the next morning. When I woke up that next day, the pain was ten times worse and I realized I needed to get to the hospital. I had to call an ambulance to come get me. Once there, an IV was started on me and they administered Dilaudid 1 mg which I didn't like because it made me feel very strange. They took me to get a CT scan of my head and numerous X-rays of my hip and shoulder. After laying there on the very uncomfortable stretcher under the blinding bright lights of the exam room, the ER doctor came in with the "news." His exact words were, "There's nothing wrong with you and you need to stop babying yourself!" I looked at him in shock. I replied, "There's too much pain everywhere for there to not be anything wrong with me." Again, he repeated, "stop babying yourself. Get moving and don't just lay around."

I couldn't move enough to go home in a cab. I requested an ambulance to return me home. A social worker came in the room to orchestrate the ride. The pain was truly getting to the point of taking my breath away. Once home, I made my way down the long hall to my bedroom. I'd soon learn that's where I'd be spending the next three months: flat in bed.

The next morning, still unable to move, I decided to call the operating room and get hold of one of the orthopedic surgeons I often worked with. I got him on the phone and told him my plight. He stated he'd go pull up my X-rays and have a look at them. He was just starting surgery so I had to wait a few hours. When he called, he started out, "No wonder you're in so much pain, you have five fractures!" How did that ER doctor miss all of this? As I'd learn many months later, he was dismissed from the hospital for his addiction problems. Enough said. So, that's how he missed all those fractures. (Don't baby myself, huh?) Fortunately, none of the fractures were displaced so no surgery was needed, but I still required complete bed rest for three months.

BECOMING AN AUTISM SUCCESS STORY

As the days went on, laying there staring up at the ceiling, I began visualizing my bones knitting back together quickly. I'd visualize this over and over. Then a strange thing happened when I had to get to the orthopedic surgeon's office at the one-month mark for follow up X-rays. That was a fiasco in itself—my disabled mom, who was on crutches, helping her daughter with five fractures into the truck from a wheelchair. Anyway, once at the office, the X-ray tech completed the numerous scans. He said, "Wow. I see you have some old fracture sites of your hip." I replied, "It happened a month ago." He continued, "No, these are old fracture sites. Healed long ago." I got a bit testy. "No, I got injured four weeks ago." He insisted, "That's impossible. These fractures all look healed."

As he wheeled me back to the exam room, the surgeon was standing in the hallway looking over my X-ray films mounted on the light boxes, looking puzzled. He then came to talk to me. That's when he informed me that I have incredibly dense bones that healed amazingly fast. He said he'd never seen anything quite like it. I still had to stay on complete bed rest for two more months, but I was well on my way to recovery. So, the question is, was that pure coincidence, or did my visualization speed up my body's recovery process? My personal opinion is that the visualization quickened the osteoblasts (cells that repair bone) to "knit" the fractures back together through the process of neuroplasticity and boosting my body's immune system. A great book on this by Dr. Norman Doidge, *The Brain's Way of Healing*, discusses "remarkable discoveries and recoveries from the frontiers of neuroplasticity."[IX] He uses stories of people who recovered from strokes, infections, head injuries, and degenerative processes through the process of visualization and neuroplasticity. Dr. Jeffrey M. Schwartz's book, *The Mind and The Brain*, discusses his research which suggests that *you* play an active role in influencing brain function by deciding where to focus your attention.

NEUROPLASTICITY

As a person who specialized in doing anesthesia for neurosurgery, I have always been fascinated with the brain. I can still recall the very first time I did a case for brain surgery, the neurosurgeon went through all the extremely tedious and meticulous steps to open the skull and expose the brain. I came around the operating table from my post at the head of the bed where the anesthesia provider stands and went to peer at the wonderous brain. With each beat of the patient's heart, the brain pulsates. I stared at it, thinking to myself how mysterious it looked: the very part of each human being which holds the feelings of love, comfort, intelligence, the ability to learn new things. Everything was right there in that pulsating, pinkish-beige, soft wonder of nature. Yes, the heart keeps us alive, but that brain is what makes us human. From that day forward, I directed my focus to learning all about the brain and spent many years administering anesthesia to patients having surgery for brain tumors, aneurysms, or other neurological problems. There are a lot of special things that must be done for such surgeries that require a lot of detail and focus. (My cup of tea.) When I was at Columbia University in New York City earning my master's in nurse anesthesia, I had to do a one-month rotation in neurosurgery at Columbia-Presbyterian Medical Center's Neuro Institute. Some of the most world-famous neurosurgeons operated there. That experience was thrilling and invaluable.

As a healthcare professional who's spent over thirty years in hospitals, I've seen many miracles of brain recovery. From patients who had strokes, severe traumatic brain injury, or neurological problems, I've witnessed recoveries that seemed impossible. The brain has tremendous resilience, or better stated, neuroplasticity. This is what allows the brain to recover, change, and regain neural pathways over time.

According to *Psychology Today*, "in neuroscience, 'plastic' means that a material has the ability to change, to be molded into different shapes. Thus, neuroplasticity is your brain's ability to alter its physical structure, to repair damaged regions, to grow new neurons and get rid of old ones, to rezone regions that performed one task and have them assume a new task, and to change the circuitry that weaves neurons into the networks that allow us to remember, feel, suffer, think, imagine, and dream."

As you can see, "whatever you ask your brain to do, it will strive to do it. Starting with employing the intention, focus on the activity, practice it in your mind, reinforce it, and you will have created the new neuronal pathways."[x]

The power of the human brain is absolutely amazing. Most people are not aware of the power they have within themselves to change, to grow, and become the most that they can become. I hope this book serves to open the door for those on the autism spectrum to tap into the powers available in their own mind. This book is also for anyone who wants to improve their life and reach their dreams. When I was a child and developed my passion for horses and riding, it was a seemingly impossible dream. I wanted it so badly, my mind couldn't rest until I figured out a way to not only earn riding time, but how to make my uncooperative body comply with my wishes to command it.

As I went on in life, I also used my visualization techniques for other areas. I used it to learn how to drive, for all aspects of my training to become a CRNA, and for social interactions. Once you decide which activity you want to learn, break it down to one step at a time. As you progress, you can later put all the pieces together to formulate the whole activity. You must also have the personal motivation to carry out the visualization process; it requires a lot of repetition and it doesn't happen overnight. It would take me a full week to "train" my mind for a new activity. You must have patience, and not get frustrated when you can't do it in a day. Rewiring your brain takes time and repetition.

One thing I truly believe is that your passion to learn something or make a positive change in yourself plays a key role in your success of carrying it out. There must be a driving force within you that so strongly wants something. Without that, you won't have the motivation it takes to do it. The more you really want something, the more effort you will put into making it happen. Having a passion for something is what ultimately separates you from others who are simply happy to stay stagnant in their ruts. Also, you must keep in mind that the level of change you are looking to make determines just how long and hard you will have to work at it. I'm not trying to make this sound discouraging. Instead, I'm trying to help you realize you must *not* be discouraged when things seem to be taking a long time. Just remember, it's a lot easier to remain stagnant and "comfortable" with your lot in life, even if that means you are unhappy. It takes a lot of personal undertaking to achieve your goals and dreams. You are the one, however, that can tap into the power that is awaiting inside you to make positive steps in your life.

SEVEN STEPS TO VISUALIZE YOUR FUTURE AND REWIRE YOUR BRAIN

Following is the "recipe" I developed over my lifetime for visualization. I cannot emphasize enough the importance of having patience for this process. I realize we now live in a world where everyone wants instant gratification; having patience will probably be a novel concept. All the greatest inventors of our time (most of which are believed to be on the autism spectrum) didn't have this immediate reward, yet they achieved great things. Many of them spent their entire lives in search of the results they eventually achieved. Their biggest virtue? Patience.

1. Clearly define what the goal is that you wish to achieve. To start out, choose a "limited" goal: start small. The critical component is that your goal is something you really are passionate about —you really, really believe this is something you want to accomplish.

2. Choose a quiet, comfortable place. It should be free of distractions of any kind. (Yes, that means you either leave your cell phone in another room or silence it.) There shouldn't be any TVs, radios, games, children, music, or anything that could pull your attention from your visualization. You need to do this in total peace and quiet, because concentration is a major component and this is your first attempt to capture your brain's attention to change your life.

3. Once in your special place, close your eyes and focus on relaxing. Concentrate on your breath; breathe in through your nose and out through your mouth. A few minutes of this goes a long way in helping you to relax. Listen to the silence and the thoughts in your head.

4. Imagine yourself exactly as you would be if you accomplished your goal. Cement that image in your mind. Focus on that from this point forward. As you are visualizing yourself achieving your goal, start adding each of the details to the image, one by one, that is needed to achieve the goal. Each detail is like a puzzle piece; start putting them together to create the whole picture. It might seem difficult and uncomfortable at first, but just be patient and go slowly. There is no rush. Take time to construct *how* you are going to achieve your goal, this "big picture" will help you to move forward. You must involve each of your senses as you want to make it totally realistic, as if you are really in the picture. Feel the weather: a cool breeze, the warmth of the sun on your back, what the wind sounds like ruffling through the leaves, the sound of water. What are any smells that may be present? Maybe it's springtime and there's beautiful flowers blooming, cascading their luscious aromas throughout the air. What is the scenery around you? Visualize the location where you want to be. As you add each element, stop for a moment to visualize the scene with the added feature. As the image in your mind gets more complex, it takes more effort to see it. After a while, this will become second nature to you. In the beginning, though, it may feel complex. Just relax.

5. If you're a verbal thinker, sometimes it is easier to include words. You might choose to write down each of the steps necessary for reaching your goal and then re-write the list several times to embed it all in your mind. After you have written down all the details, read the words out loud several times or rehearse them in your head. Do whatever feels comfortable. It is only through repetition that the brain imprints the reality of your visualization. Perhaps you can think of other steps you think

you will need to do to reach your goal. Articulate them, as well. If you define the actions needed to get there, you are projecting that into your brain's memory. I like to use 4" x 6" index cards and organize them in a little plastic box. It helps me clear my thoughts and feel organized.

6. Repeat the same visualization a few times a day, for short periods around ten minutes or so. Each time you do this, always start out by visualizing yourself reaching your goal. This will become integrated into your life and your brain's definition, because your brain "interpret[s] imagery as equivalent to a real-life action."[XI]

7. Only visualize your goal with positive steps and a positive outcome. You are training your brain to reach your goal. It is highly critical that you never allow yourself to include any negative thoughts in this entire process. If you do, you will be setting yourself up for failure. It is fine to visualize several different ways to achieve your goal, but never include anything negative.

Depending upon the difficulty of your goal, it may take more time than you initially thought for changes occur. This is not like hypnosis, which is time-limited, nor is it an "improvement" process, like a diet. You are rewiring your brain, which will be permanent if the firing neurons sufficiently link together. You should continue to visualize your goal until it happens, which may take time. The more complex and seemingly impossible, the longer it will take you to get there. I once had a dream of getting a flight in an F-15 fighter jet. As you will read a bit further along in the book, you'll find it took me seven years to achieve that goal. But I never gave up. And I can tell you, it was worth all the visualization and time, as it was one of the most thrilling experiences of my life!

Once you understand how to do this, it opens your mind and your life to possibilities you never even imagined! Cherish your brain and realize the power you have within yourself. It's all up to you. The power of visualization is there waiting for you. It is *your* future!

THE POWER OF VISUALIZATION IS AVAILABLE TO ALL

There are two types of visualization: "outcome visualization," which involves you actually envisioning yourself achieving your goal, and "process visualization," which involves visualizing the steps to your goal. Between both of them, you will have a clear picture of how your goal will feel and look. Remember, visualization doesn't simply make your goals happen. You must be willing to work hard and practice it over and over and maintain the patience necessary for it all to come together.

The strength of visualization is relatively simple in theory. You can use your imagination to trick your brain, because your brain doesn't differentiate between physical and imaginary activity. It brings the latest and most frequent version of the event in your memory to reality. The old is eliminated; the newest becomes the definition of the activity.

The advantage of visualization is that it involves no expense. It is an individualized "project" that you are in control of. It doesn't involve drugs, physical operations, or any dangerous procedures—just you and your dreams.

AGE DOESN'T MATTER

Without a doubt, there is an avenue to rewire the brains of adults. It can seem more difficult as you get older, because you've packed in so many experiences and knowledge already, but don't be discouraged. How do I know it can work for individuals on the autism spectrum? Because my husband, Abraham, also used visualization and neuroplasticity to produce an incredible change!

When I first met Abraham, it was like finding a person on a deserted island in the middle of the Pacific Ocean. He had been living a very sheltered, isolated life. He didn't understand any idiomatic expressions. He didn't know how to do much of anything other than make a cup of coffee. He knew nothing of the outside world or how to live in it and he wasn't capable of fending for himself. Family members referred to him as "disabled" and "handicapped" right in front of him, which he believed, thus he believed he was totally incapable of accomplishing anything.

We had a perfect chemistry together from our first hug, and we always work as a team. Because of my experiences with visualization, I was able to teach him to use it to become independent. Just as my mom taught me to recognize the power of the mind, I taught him. It wasn't something that happened overnight. It has taken four years to get him to where he's at now, which is light-years from where he was then.

Many individuals with autism learn differently than others. They are not dumb; they just need to learn in a different way. If I tried to explain to him how to do something, the words would go through one ear and out the other. Lots of words are nothing but a jumbled-up blur to him. However, if I first demonstrated something to him and then had him visualize it in his mind many times, he would embed it in his brain and perform it on his own. First, we'd

CHAPTER 2

think of an activity and I'd do it to show him how; then we'd create all the steps to accomplish it. Next, we'd break it down into the individual steps, visualizing each one over and over and over. Finally, we'd put all the pieces back together to create the whole picture.

Through visualization and the magic of neuroplasticity, Abraham rewired his brain to become a fully functional adult. Yes, he has autism, but he evolved into being independent and doing all the things that any neurotypical adult can do. He got his driver's license, he works at a professional job as an AutoCAD draftsman, he can run a household, grocery shop, cook gourmet meals, pay bills, and has mastered all the other activities of daily living.

Cooking was a big challenge. I've never taught anyone to cook before, so I realized I needed to start from scratch. Food safety was the very first thing he needed to learn. Having had food poisoning twice in my life, once necessitating hospitalization, I know the seriousness of food safety. He knew nothing: things like handwashing prior to any food preparation, not rinsing raw chicken in the sink, not touching raw meat with bare hands, not placing those things on a cutting board that is used for any other purpose, etc. He wrote down each item, then visualized each one for a week. To be sure he understood it all, we discussed each concept while he demonstrated it. He wrote out each concept on an index card to aid in the visualization process. He also placed each index card in a little plastic box designed especially for the cards (which you can get at any office supply store) and organized them for the specific activities.

Abraham read over the cards each day, did the visualization of each step, and a week later had it all solidified in his brain. The next stage was having him observe me actually doing food preparation. I kept talking to a minimum, so all his attention could be maintained on seeing what I was doing. From peeling an onion and dicing it, to putting zucchini through a food processor to make it into noodles, I showed him everything. He had to incorporate those safety skills he already learned to be able to continue on to the next stage, but it was easy because his brain was already rewired and able to quickly access those actions. For example, first he washed his hands, then washed the zucchini. He followed all the safety steps to use our food processor, put the zucchini into it, and operate the machine. Before he did all of that, he visualized each step until, in his mind, he already had done it numerous times. When he actually performed the actions, the process went very smoothly.

Next, he learned how to sauté, grill, steam, and bake using the same pattern. As Abraham describes it, his mind recorded me demonstrating each process. So, what was the most difficult thing for him to learn? Processing words. He can replicate anything I show him but if I describe it verbally, it isn't going to happen. Once he sees it, he can visualize it over and over and over, rewiring his brain through the neuroplasticity capability each one of us has.

Fast-forward four years later, Abraham now cooks exactly like I do, which is quite extensively. My mom taught me to cook and bake from scratch when I was a young child, so I can do it very well. Visualization and neuroplasticity went a long way in enabling Abraham to reach this level of competency.

Abraham received his driver's license after using visualization for the whole process, which included taking the actual driving test. He had to visualize having a stranger sitting in the passenger seat while he accomplished it, as the employee from the motor vehicle office would be sitting in the passenger seat grading him throughout the test. Abraham was used to me sitting in the passenger seat, so I had him visualize someone else. Abraham knew the basics of driving a vehicle when we first met but did not have his driver's license. He was too timid and not comfortable at all behind the wheel. I orchestrated the process for him to learn and get comfortable and confident driving. We took things very slowly, one step at a time with a lot of repetition. An individual with autism isn't going to learn to drive like others, so the method needs to be one which accommodates special needs. I have a great presentation on driving that I do at conferences and share this process with others on the autism spectrum and their parents.

He is now a fully functioning adult on the autism spectrum and has gained total independence, which gave him confidence in himself. He went from rock-bottom self-esteem to now having personal confidence, pride in his work, and the knowledge that he can set his mind on something and accomplish it by visualizing his way there.

> *"Far from being fixed, the brain is a highly dynamic*
> *structure, which undergoes significant change, not only*
> *as it develops, but also throughout the entire lifespan."*
> — *Moheb Costandi* [XII]

Every parent worries what will become of their child with autism. Utilizing visualization could be their answer. It's not just for those on the autism spectrum—visualization is for anyone who wants to have a better life—but it is particularly relevant to those with autism who have strong attention to detail, a desire for acceptance and understanding, visual thinking, and the ability to capture sensory experiences. Those should be viewed as attributes, not detriments. A young child or an older adult can change his or her life through visualization, whether the person has autism or is neurotypical.

HOW TO STOP ANXIETY
WITH VISUALIZATION

Anxiety is something very common to most on the autism spectrum, myself included. It isn't just in your head. Anxiety causes many physical symptoms ranging from simply annoying to those which can lead to serious ill health effects. These symptoms can affect an individual's life in many ways, including things like sleep, appetite, job performance, relationships, and more. Many people are probably familiar with the "fight or flight" response. When you get anxious over something, your body instantly secretes adrenalin, the stress hormone. Unfortunately, for a person who suffers from chronic anxiety, this stress response is happening every day, many times a day. Cortisol, another stress hormone, is also secreted when the adrenalin is pumped out. These hormones will increase a person's blood sugar levels and increase their triglycerides (blood fats).

For those who suffer from anxiety, there are two things you need to do. You must first find a way to decrease your anxiety in the moment, and second, to come up with a long-term plan to control it. The more intense your anxiety, the more it negatively affects your quality of life. Visualization is a tool for managing anxiety. By transferring yourself mentally to a peaceful, relaxing, and safe environment, you can calm your mind and body.

My suggestion for using visualization for decreasing anxiety is to follow my seven-step visualization guide with the goal of decreasing your anxiety. Learning to practice those steps in a calm, quiet place will help in the process. You will need to focus on sending away the stressors and allowing your entire body to relax. In essence, you will be teaching yourself how to relax all over again. That is half the battle of decreasing anxiety.

By learning how to relax and visualize your anxiety receding, you will be doing something positive for your health, wellness, and overall happiness.

EXAMPLES OF SCENES FOR YOUR VISUALIZATION

I am going to give several examples of setting up your visualization scenes in your mind. These are places I'd like to transport myself to. You can think of where you'd like to "go" for *your* visualization. I've never been to Lake Louise in British Columbia, but I've seen enough photos of it to know that's where I'd love to be!

I envision that I'm in a small log cabin overlooking Lake Louise in Banff, British Columbia. Evening is setting in, and it's snowing outside. I'm looking out a huge window with an expansive view of the lake, the mountains, and towering pines. I'm sitting next to the rustic fieldstone fireplace, feeling the warmth of a fire and listening to the crackling sound and occasional popping from the wood burning. I also feel the warmth of the old-fashioned mug I'm holding with both my hands, fingers wrapped around it, as I slowly sip the steaming coffee I freshly brewed and savor the rich aroma. I am feeling very relaxed, all the tension in my whole body has drained away, leaving me feeling very peaceful. As I watch the nighttime set in, I begin to see the northern lights appear across the sky. It looks as if a sheer, shimmering curtain is gently moving in a breeze. Beautiful shades of light green, pink, and lavender are all moving in a spectacular display of the phenomenon also called the aurora borealis. I am mesmerized by this spectacle of nature. Each of my senses are overwhelmed. All of my anxiety is long gone.

I imagine this scene, and "stay" there for fifteen or twenty minutes. I feel like I'm really there—so much so that I look forward to visiting often!

Here's another scene. Pensacola Beach, Florida, has beautiful white pristine beaches and turquoise water of the Gulf of Mexico. I start by imagining myself laying on a lounge chair right near the water with a large umbrella shading me from the sun. I have my legs off the side of the chair with my feet nestled into the warm sand. It is the same texture as cornstarch, and it's a very cozy sensation. I look out to the Gulf, watching the turquoise and emerald green water generate waves which come rolling onto the sand, capped with white crests. I love the sound as the water rushes toward me, just a few inches deep. Seagulls are drifting on the air currents above the water and just over my head, crying out occasionally. I'm savoring the fresh aroma of the salt air created by the sea. The breeze on my face feels calming, and I release the tension of my forehead, between my eyebrows, and feel my face relax. I am feeling relaxed from head to toe. My breathing is slow and peaceful. I could stay there for hours!

With these scenes I've just shown you, I hope you get the picture of how easy it is to create an image in your mind that fills all your senses. Be sure to pick somewhere you really want to be, whether or not you have ever been there before. Just be sure that there are no negative thoughts or events associated with the place you will go to. Also, remember that you will need to do this over and over numerous times until it becomes etched in your mind. Don't give up if at first it seems overwhelming. In fact, a great way to start is to add one sensory item at a time, building as you go. For example, just envision the sights of the place, noticing all details. The next time see those sights plus add any sounds. Then, after that, smell any special aromas. Then add any special sensations. This way, it won't seem so overwhelming to try and visualize the entire scene at once.

MY VISUALIZATION

I used my own version of visualization as a child, when I was only just discovering how to do it. Now, professional athletes of today are using these methods through the coaching of sports psychologists. It is all clearly backed by science and research, and even brain scans that prove this method works. You will feel very empowered for each step of improvement that you make. Keep in mind that the level of your improvement will be directly proportionate to the effort you put into the process. If you want something badly enough, you can do it—no matter how long it takes. You are on a personal journey, so there's no rush. Little accomplishments may seem just that, little, but eventually they add up to reach your goal.

CHAPTER 3

HORSE THERAPY AND AUTISM

"I wish more kids could ride horses today. People and animals are supposed to be together. We spent quite a long time evolving together, and we used to be partners."

— DR. TEMPLE GRANDIN

CHAPTER 3

I t was on the back of a horse where I discovered I have the ability for laser focus and visualization. I was mesmerized by the cadence of the horse's hoof beats as he walked along. I would count the *one-two-three-four, one-two-three-four* rhythm and begin to focus on the fact that it made my hips move in synchrony with his steps. I would listen to that sound, feel my body moving with the horse, and tune out the rest of the world. I began to visualize that I was watching the horse move, to see each step as if I were watching a movie. The movement of the horse transfers the physical imprint into your body, which takes you into an entirely different zone. Movement is somehow connected to strong visualization.

Several years ago, I heard about therapeutic riding, but only recently learned of hippotherapy. Hippotherapy is a form of therapy that utilizes horseback riding as treatment. Essentially, the movement of the horse can help the balance, coordination, and overall strength of the rider. During the writing of this book, as I researched each of these avenues of horse therapy, I realized that I basically had some form of each of them. Even though there wasn't an actual physical therapist, an occupational therapist, or speech-language pathologist at the stable, they came in different forms. Whether it was the riding instructors, the stable hands, the veterinarians, farriers, or others, they all enabled me to get the "therapy" I needed.

BECOMING A WORKING STUDENT

Because I came from a very poor family, horse riding lessons were far from something my parents could afford. Except for my first set of group lessons when I was in the fifth grade, the rest of my riding career was earned from my own hard work. In order to attend those riding lessons, I would need to leave school early each Friday for eight weeks. My mom went to ask the principal of my elementary school if she could get me out at two o'clock instead of three o'clock for those eight weeks. I wasn't the world's best student back in those days, so when she asked him (with me at her side) he instantly replied, "Oh, sure! Anita is never going to amount to anything anyway, so it doesn't matter." To this day, I can still picture him standing there, saying that. I love to share that story, as I've heard many parents tell me of some "professional" telling them the same thing about their child. I tell them simply to ignore such comments and forge on.

I became a working student at a big stable near my home. I started working there when I was twelve. The deal was that you earned riding time and lessons in exchange for working at the stable. The majority of that work was in the form of mucking out stalls. From then on, every summer, weekend, and holiday was spent at the stable. Mucking out stalls would become a normal way of life for me. It was hard physical labor, but it was also a labor of love. It gave me the opportunity to spend time with each horse in their stall, studying their every move. They studied me, as well. Each one was curious of me and would come over, sniff me, and typically put their velvety soft nose against me. It was a magical bond that was very sacred to me. That bond was also present when I was in the saddle. I could get even the most unruly and emotionally troubled horses to perform for me like no one else could. Several years ago, I happened to think of one of my horse buddies from back in my working student days. I looked her up online, and there she was. I sent her a message and asked if she remembered me. Sure enough, she did. I then asked her what she recalled about me. I was convinced she was going to write back stating she remembered how hard I worked, that I mucked out more stalls than everyone else and got to ride a lot. Instead, she wrote back and said how jealous she always was of me, because it was obvious that I had some kind of magical bond with every horse and could get them to do things no one else could.

I eventually became in charge of the school horses, which included tending to the tack room filled with about twenty saddles and bridles. I'd spend hours cleaning each and every one with a tiny sponge and saddle soap. I'd then use leather conditioner to keep the saddles and bridles in good, soft condition. It was very peaceful to be in that tack room all by myself, listening to the horses munching hay and the birds singing while I was learning to manage my time and work. I had to keep track of which horses needed to be ready for lessons at specific times, what time I needed to feed them, clean their stalls, or be ready to walk out a hot horse returning from a lesson. I was ready for anything; this job was teaching me life skills, yet I didn't even know it at the time.

The bottom line is that when I walked into that stable all those years ago, I felt trapped inside a shell, unable to join in life like everyone else. I was uncoordinated, timid, had zero self-esteem and was unable to talk to anyone besides my mom. When I left to go to college, I was a different person: self-confident, coordinated, balanced. I had management skills, work skills, I knew how to interact with anyone, and I had discovered my ability to laser focus. Horses saved my life.

WHAT IS HIPPOTHERAPY?

On the official Equestrian Therapy website, they state, "Hippotherapy is a form of speech, physical and occupational therapy or treatment using a horse as a healing medium. The characteristic movements of the horse are used to carefully render sequential sensory and motor input, and improve sensory processing and neurological function of a subject ... Hippotherapy relies mostly on horse movement for the treatment of people with mental or physical disabilities."[XIII]

Throughout all the years I rode, I had the opportunity to ride hundreds of different horses. Each one had their own movement, depending on the breed, size, and body type. By riding all those different horses, I experienced many types of movement, all of which helped in the therapeutic effects it all had on my mind and body. There are so many forms of equestrian therapy that riders can benefit from.

1. **Therapeutic Riding** – "This form of therapy offers a unique way to develop flexibility, balance, coordination, and muscle strength." Following is a great description of benefits for the individual from equestriantherapy.org:

    - "Physically: The horse's movement has a dynamic effect on the rider's body
    - Sensorial: The horse and riding environment offers a wide variety of sensory input to the participants
    - Emotionally: Overcoming fear and anxiety and the ability to achieve riding skills help riders increase self-esteem
    - Cognitively: The horse provides a strong motivator for riders. Riding sessions incorporate activities and games on horseback designed to help each rider achieve specific goals
    - Socially: The riding program and all activities provide an excellent opportunity for participants to interact with their peers, program volunteers and with the staff in a positive and enjoyable environment."[XIV]

2. **Equine Facilitated Learning** – EFL is a method now widely used in the United States and is still increasing in popularity.

It is the concept that people can benefit in many positive ways by spending time with horses and can apply the lessons they learn with their horses to benefit them in everyday life. Because horses are so perceptive and responsive, a person can learn a lot about their body language and self-awareness from interacting with the animal. As a result, one will almost certainly experience increased confidence and self-esteem, have better communication with others, and more fulfilling relationships. They will develop increased knowledge about the cause and effects of their behavior. Responsibility for a living, breathing animal can always allow the person to feel a greater empathy for others.

3. **Equine Facilitated Psychotherapy** – An interesting article in *Perspectives in Psychiatric Care* stated, "This is a growing trend in the field of psychology that allows horses to be an integral part of the treatment of youths, adults, and families that struggle with mental health issues. This unique therapy provides opportunities to enhance self-awareness, develop feelings of self-love, and allow people to grow, progress, and heal. It is available as a viable alternative or supplement to traditional therapy methods." [XV]

As you can see, there are numerous forms of therapy that horses can provide to humans. Whichever one you look at, they all have an effect on the mind, body, and soul. A wonderful quote by Winston Churchill says, "There is something about the outside of a horse that is good for the inside of a man."

HOW A CHILD WITH AUTISM CAN BENEFIT FROM HIPPOTHERAPY

For thousands of years, the human-animal connection has proven to be effective in creating an emotional, healing bond. This unique bond is recognized more and more, with several universities now offering special degrees and certificates related to the human-animal connection. Tufts University has the Tufts Institute for Human-Animal Interaction. Tufts also has a veterinary school where the human-animal connection is also recognized and addressed. The University of Denver has the Institute for Human-Animal Connection, where numerous certificate programs are offered regarding the human-animal connection.

With hippotherapy, the assistance of physical therapists, occupational therapists, and speech-language pathologists are utilized. Other forms of therapy are also highly effective due to the motor, emotional, and sensory sensations that come with riding a horse.

DEVELOPING THE EMOTIONAL BOND AND COGNITIVE SKILLS

Individuals on the autism spectrum have difficulty bonding emotionally to others. It is extremely difficult for them to make eye contact or to communicate and express the way they're feeling. Horse therapy enables the individual with autism to experience physical communication with a living, breathing creature. They can brush the horse, hug them, pet them, and learn to care for them. As they start providing that care, feelings will develop and they will build an emotional bond with the horse. This can lead to development of social and communication skills that can be used in life with other people.

CHAPTER 3

It is not uncommon that individuals on the autism spectrum have difficulty comprehending directions that others would find easy. Working with horses is a fun activity that makes it easier for them to grasp the concept of, follow, and remember directions. The individual also has to give direction to the horse, which provides more opportunity to communicate instructions. Cognitive skills will naturally improve as the sessions go on.

EVIDENCE-BASED RESEARCH

There is research being done to validate the positive results obtained from therapeutic riding and hippotherapy for children on the autism spectrum. Robin Gabriels, PsyD at the University of Colorado School of Medicine, is interested in diagnostic assessment and treatment of youth with autism spectrum disorders. Her research focuses on evaluating the outcomes of animal-assisted interventions for the ASD community. Her latest study, Project Aim, is piloting a coding measure of behavior change in children with autism spectrum disorder from pre- to post-therapeutic horseback riding.

As this book is being written, Colorado State University is breaking ground for the Temple Grandin Equine Center. According to CSU, they "aspire to create a new home for equine-assisted activities and therapies; a place where individuals with physical, emotional, and developmental challenges can heal, where therapists can treat, where students can learn, and where scientists can research."[XVI] They will honor the contributions of the facility's namesake, Temple Grandin, as it showcases the healing powers of the equine species in assisting people with specific individual needs.

Everyone knows what an important role horses played in Temple's life. As she says, "Horses were basically my salvation. If I had not been able to go down to the horse barn and clean the stalls, I would have been miserable."[XVII]

Research into the effects of equine therapy are not yet that abundant. However, I can tell you for sure that each and every horse I rode, and every hour I spent working around them, served as my therapy. I feel entirely confident to say that my experience with horses made me a functional, independent, and thriving adult. I encourage parents of children with autism to seek out equine therapy for your child. I also encourage adults with autism to find an equine therapy program near them—you cannot age out of the magic of horse therapy.

THE HORSE BOY

While working on this book I came across a very unique story: the story about "the horse boy," and the positive effects of dressage on children with autism. Elgin, Texas is home of New Trails, headquarters of The Horse Boy Foundation, The Horse Boy Method, and the horse boy himself, Rowan Isaacson, who has autism. His father, Rupert Isaacson, is an award-winning author, humanitarian, and dressage rider. In a quest to help his son, Rupert and his wife Kristin Neff, a university professor and author, packed up and took their son Rowan to Mongolia to ride across the land on horseback. Once back home and back in the saddle, Rupert discovered that the more collected (controlled) the horse's gaits became, the more Rowan would speak.

Rupert found there to be a connection between riding a horse in collection and getting kids on the autism spectrum to communicate. From that, he developed New Trails, where "The Horse Boy Method" is taught. People travel from all over the world to learn this method. It is endorsed by some of the biggest names in the horse world including "Linda Tellington-Jones (TTouch Method), Anna Ross Davies (British International Dressage Rider), Bernard Sachse (French gold-medal dressage Paralympian), and Alfredo Hernandez (California-based piaffe/passage guru)."[XVIII]

Early on, Rupert searched for adults with autism who became successful and found Dr. Temple Grandin. He went to interview her, basically asking Temple how his son can become just like her, and she gave him great advice, opposite of what his son's behavioral therapists were recommending. Dr. Grandin's advice was what started making a difference. Dr. Grandin told Rupert to do three things:

1. "Follow the child (physically, emotionally, and intellectually);
2. Work outside in nature as much as possible, where there are no bad sensory triggers;
3. Let Rowan move, move, move, because most kids on the autism spectrum are kinetic learners."[XIX]

Once Rupert began following Temple's advice, it proved to be immediately successful. It all began one day while out in the woods, as Grandin advised. Rowan spotted his neighbors herd of horses and ran in amongst them. Rupert froze. Rupert was a lifelong horseman and ex-professional horse trainer. He had purposefully been keeping Rowan away from horses because he was worried his son would be unsafe around them. Instead, he witnessed something extraordinary. All the horses had backed away from Rowan, who was squirming and babbling, laying on his back among the horses. A mare named Betsy, the boss of the herd, slowly came over to Rowan. She lowered her head and began licking and chewing with her lips. It was clear there was something special happening between Betsy and Rowan.

Rupert asked his neighbor if they could ride Betsy and, for the next three years through the woods and fields of central Texas, they did. It was there on Betsy's back where Rowan began to talk; first only in the saddle, then in everyday life situations. He also began to engage with his environment and other people.

According to Rupert, when a person rides a horse in collected gaits such as the collected canter, piaffe, passage, or canter pirouettes, the hip-rocking rhythm causes the human body to produce the feel-good hormone oxytocin. That would explain why I was literally addicted to riding those collected gaits (as you'll learn later). I would feel total freedom and euphoria throughout the ride and for hours afterward.

New Trails has numerous courses available and there's even a huge guest house right on the property where families can stay. It's not only for children with autism, but for trainers to come and learn the Horse Boy Method to take back to their country to teach at their facilities. I can attest to the fact that all of these methods truly *do* work in helping to get a child with autism functioning and ultimately working toward being a self-advocate.[xx]

GET INVOLVED!

For all these amazing benefits, there is one minor drawback: hippotherapy can be expensive. Luckily, there are several organizations that offer scholarships and other helpful options that can make this effective therapy fit into a budget. Of course, there's always the possibility to become a working student and do work in return for riding time like I did (that is, if a person is lucky enough to live near a stable which offers that type of opportunity). Whatever it takes to makes it happen, I highly suggest the effort is made to get the individual with autism involved with horse therapy in some way.

It must be remembered that hippotherapy is not merely recreation for those with disabilities. It has specific therapeutic goals. It is a tool that takes advantage of a horse's natural rhythmic and repetitive movements to help improve patients' muscle tone, balance, posture, coordination, strength, flexibility and cognitive skills. Also, hippotherapy—despite containing the word "therapy"—is not provided by equine therapists. Physical therapists, occupational therapists, and speech-language pathologists provide hippotherapy. These therapists are healthcare providers. They receive years of schooling and clinical supervision and pass board exams before receiving their license. They then complete additional continuing education before incorporating horses into therapy.

SAFETY ALWAYS COMES FIRST

I must address safety in this book. By no means do I want to scare anyone, but safety must always come first. I will say that engaging in horse riding can be dangerous when riding on your own. When you do extreme activities—jumping, cross-country events, polo, or any type of horse sport— you can get injured, even killed. For the purpose of horse therapy and hippotherapy, however, it's unlikely that you'll get injured. There are multiple people in attendance with the individual receiving the therapy who are specially trained to handle all situations. The horses utilized for therapy are very carefully chosen based on their temperament, gait, and personality. Their age, health, conformation, and training are also determining factors. The movement the horse produces is used to affect change in the individual receiving hippotherapy; if the horse is unsound, unfit, stiff, or is reluctant to move freely forward, the movement produced would be asymmetrical or of poor quality for therapy. Each horse has a different movement. As a person who has ridden hundreds of different horses in my lifetime, I can attest to this fact! Some horses have huge gaits, and their walk is very stimulating to the vestibular system. Some have a walk that produces barely perceptible movement, which would make them undesirable for hippotherapy.

CERTIFIED VS. UNCERTIFIED

A word of caution to anyone shopping for equine therapy or hippotherapy: in order to be confident that you or your child will be receiving the correct and safe version, be sure to investigate that the organization is truly a valid one with certified therapists. Unfortunately, there will always be a group who advertises themselves as equine therapy, horse therapy, etc. who has no formal training, or horses that are not safe for therapy.

CHAPTER 4

HORSE THERAPY AND HARD WORK

"You can't wait around for opportunities to come your way. You must seek them out and make them happen."

— ANITA LESKO

CHAPTER 4

I f you've ever sat on a horse, there is one thing you know for sure: there are lots of moving parts! Not only is the horse moving, but you must also learn to control your whole body to move along with it. This all takes major balance and coordination, neither of which I had prior to horseback riding. Riding a horse can help improve balance and spatial orientation and is particularly beneficial for those who have trouble with those senses, whether they're on the spectrum or not. Plus, it's fun, so it doesn't feel like "therapy" even though the rider is building these skills.

I have very few photos of me jumping horses because we couldn't afford a camera, so we just relied on others to give us any photos they happened to capture of me in mid-air. I have one photo in particular that, to this day, I look at in total amazement. I used to ride a horse who was quite the handful—but boy, could she jump. Standing at only fourteen hands, she was an Anglo-Arab, all white, and I swear she had wings on her feet to be so small yet capable of jumping so high. The photo was taken at a big horse show where I was showing her. There were three classes for me that day, and each round they raised the fences higher and higher. The last jump-off was against a rider that, years later, was in the Olympics. The fences were raised so high I couldn't see over them as I was galloping toward them. My mom was begging me not to jump that high. She was so scared I'd get seriously injured, or worse. I wouldn't hear of it and kept going—and came in first place! When I had my mind set on something, that was it. What an obnoxious kid I was!

MASTERING TOTAL BODY CONTROL

Riding a horse takes a major amount of coordination. Jumping over six-foot fences takes even more. I'm going to describe in explicit details exactly what is going on in the process of it all. Of course, I was able to get to this degree of control not only through all my years of riding, but the hard physical labor I did all those years in the stables. It all came together in a pinnacle of performance. It proves the true healing power of the horse and everything involved with their care, and also the power of visualization and neuroplasticity.

There are, indeed, lots of moving parts to keep track of. As you are galloping toward a jump, you must be in total control of the horse. It must be a slow gallop (or, I should say, a fast canter) yet still controlled. You must visually determine the distance to the obstacle and slow down or speed up depending on that distance. How you bring the horse to it will determine how successfully he can jump it. If you pilot him incorrectly, he may well refuse to jump and slam on the "breaks," possibly resulting in you flying over his head and having a bad fall. This visualization process is developed over many years—it took that long for me, at least. Obviously, when you start learning to jump it's over tiny jumps like cross-rails, about eighteen inches in height.

Now that you have your eyes fixed on the upcoming obstacle, you need to slow the horse down, collecting his energy. You must be in complete control of every inch of your body in addition to being in control of every inch of the horse's body, too. Your chin is up, you are looking at the jump. Your heels are pushing downwards in the stirrups, your feet are parallel with the horse's sides, and a straight line drawn down would have your knees in alignment with your toes. Your body weight sinks down through your heels. Your behind is just up out of the saddle a bit, keeping your weight off his back and preparing to go over the jump. Your back is straight, not hunching. Your hands are holding the reins which control the horse, and they are close together with thumbs upward. Your arms are relaxed yet in control, following along the reins with the natural movement of the horse as he gallops, maintaining fluid movement. The fence is looming closer. Instinctively, you recognize the crucial moment when the horse takes that final stride and begins thrusting upwards to sail over the top of the jump. Going along with that motion, your upper body lifts upwards and forwards, and you follow the stretching of his head and neck with the reins, allowing him total freedom to jump. Your hands follow along with the crest of his neck, your fingers maintaining contact against his neck as you soar over the fence. Your legs are tight on his sides, your behind is now completely up and out of the saddle with your weight still sinking down through your heels. You are looking ahead, focused looking between his ears. As he is flying through the air, cresting over the top, your body must begin instantly preparing to descend for landing. All of this is happening in but a few seconds. As the descent begins, you start shifting your upper body more upright, but not completely. You maintain that jumping position until his hooves touch the ground and you are galloping toward the next jump. Then you resume the basic jumping position and collect his gallop to be in full control as you prepare to do it all over again. It's a very thrilling feeling to ride a horse over huge obstacles. You feel very empowered and confident, which carries over into your life outside the saddle. I was quite the daredevil on a horse. Looking back, I can't believe I did all that crazy stuff!

Aside from acting like Evil Knievel, the bigger picture is that I went from being a severely uncoordinated kid to maintaining such a high level of total body control through all my "therapy" with the horses. Years and years of riding built my core strength; improved my coordination, balance, gross and fine motor skills, and equilibrium; and developed my proprioception, speech and language, and self-esteem. I shudder to think of where I'd be today if I hadn't developed my passion for horses; I will boldly say I would never have become successful in life and found true happiness. Yes, it's all that and a bag of chips! The horses were my teachers and therapists, and I hope this book will inspire others on the autism spectrum to seek out equine-assisted therapy in whatever form they can find near them. My testimony within the pages here will hopefully convince others to follow in my footsteps.

In addition to the development of everything listed above, working at the stable also served in the development of learning how to work. It taught me how to take orders from a boss, how to manage my time, how to be considerate of others, how to get a job done, proper work ethics, and overall prepared me for life, a successful career, relationships with others, and even marriage.

LEARNING BY WATCHING

When I first became a working student at the big stable near my home in New Jersey, I spent a lot of time studying horses and their behavior. I spent equally as much time studying the people at the barn. That included the workers tending to the horses, the riding instructors, the office staff, the students coming for their riding lessons, and those very lucky ones who owned their own horses. There was much to be learned from all this. My brain is like a sponge, absorbing everything I see and hear. In addition to learning how to work and ride, I was also learning social skills and, simply, human behavior. I recognized that they all operated very differently than I did. They made endless facial expressions, as if they were trying to simply "talk" with their faces. It looked a little like sign language to me, only using their faces instead of hands.

I'd watch for hours the stable hands mucking out the stalls. I'd watch every little detail of how they held the pitchfork, how they use the tines to pick up the piles of manure and toss it into the wheelbarrow. I observed just how high they'd load that wheelbarrow with the mound of soiled shavings. I'd watch how they then pushed the wheelbarrow down the aisle, and up the precarious ramp to the dumpster located outside the huge doorway. I watched very closely how they walked out to the end of the ramp and then slowly lifted the handles forward to dump the contents into the dumpster. Over and over, I visualized myself doing every single thing they did. I'd imagine it as if I was actually doing it, then I'd visualize it as if I were watching a movie of myself doing the work. Then I felt like I actually had really done it. I was pretty scared of that rickety ramp as all it was made of was some well-worn plywood over two boards. It was maybe three feet wide. It spanned from the doorway up to the edge of the dumpster, which was about twelve feet in length. I can still recall how scared I was when I first saw that ramp. Knowing how clumsy I was, I was worried that if I lost my balance I'd fall in! When I visualized things, I realized it was important to imagine things just how I wanted it to go and to keep it positive.

After watching all of this for a day or so, I simply walked over to an empty wheelbarrow, grabbed a pitchfork, and went over to a stall whose occupant was outside in the paddock. I began slowly at first, making sure I did everything exactly as I observed the workers doing it. I found it very peaceful. I listened to all the various birds singing, the sound of horses in their stalls munching on their hay, the clip-clop as horses were led down the concrete aisleway. I loved the smell of all the horses, the hay, the feed, everything. It was intoxicating.

I felt like I was brought to life. The stable was awakening all my senses, allowing me to experience life on a level I didn't know existed. I felt a sense of giddiness inside. It was the first time in my life I felt truly happy: free from the torment of the bullies, free from feeling trapped inside myself.

I had started talking when I was two, but only at home to my mom. I wouldn't say a word to anyone else. But that all changed once I became a working student. Then I wanted to talk to others (about horses, of course). This new experience got me to come out of my shell and begin interacting with others. Looking back, I guess all those people recognized there was something very unusual about me, yet they seemed to overlook it. I think they saw that I had a very special bond with the horses, and that was good enough for them. Everyone was always happy to teach me something new, especially safety advice. I suspect they also recognized my clumsiness and watched out for me. Safety around horses has always remained of the utmost importance to me. I can still recall the stable hand who came up to me on my first day on the job to help me understand how to navigate the ramp up to the dumpster. He had me push the loaded wheelbarrow down the aisle to the doorway where the ramp was. He explained that I must take small steps as I'm pushing up the ramp and showed me where to stop once at the top. He continued, saying to slowly raise the handles upward and then forward, being careful not to reach out away from myself too far or else it would throw me off balance and I might fall forward. I had been watching him and the others doing it multiple times and had visualized the sequence in my mind dozens of times. I felt ready to do it. With him standing right there, I took a deep breath, picked up the handles of the wheelbarrow, and went up the ramp. I took tiny steps to be sure I stayed right in the center of the ramp. I stopped at the necessary point and successfully dumped my first load of shavings into the dumpster. I felt very proud of myself, but the next trick was getting back down the ramp. Ever so slowly, I walked backward, inching my way back to safety. Neil, the worker, was still there giving moral support as I crept backward.

Once back on the concrete I was ready to go for round two, so I headed back to find another unoccupied stall. For the first week I only cleaned the stalls without the horse in them. After that, I would seek out the stalls with the horse in it. Through observation, I learned how to slowly slide open the big stall door and immediately position the wheelbarrow across the doorway so the horse couldn't walk out. I noticed that Neil and the other two guys kept an eye on me and what I was doing. They didn't talk much, just occasionally. They would comment to me that I work very hard. They would also report all of my work to the two riding instructors, who would then give me riding lessons and free riding according to how much I did. As you might guess, I worked harder and faster than any of the other working students to earn lots of time in the saddle.

As the days and weeks went on, my skills at stall cleaning were increasing. I was getting faster and more efficient at it. At first, I couldn't load too much into the wheelbarrow, as my coordination wasn't very good and it would teeter too much if filled to capacity. I'd end up spilling too much along the way down the aisle. It wasn't long before I was able to load it up like Neil did.

GETTING STRONG AND
LEARNING BALANCE

It was already a month into my first summer at the barn as a working student and I felt stronger with each passing day. I also noticed I wasn't quite as clumsy as I was prior to starting there. That made me smile to myself. I continued working as fast and hard as I could. The two riding instructors talked to me about starting out my riding "career" doing what they called lunge-line lessons. They explained that this would help me to develop good balance and would help me become the best rider I could be. I was thrilled to hear that. Little did I know it would be the therapy I so desperately needed and would become the building blocks for the rest of my life.

I didn't understand what they were talking about, so I went down to the indoor riding arena to watch one of these lessons being given to another student. The instructor, Marsha, had a thirty-five-foot-long line called a lunge line. One end was attached to the halter, which went over the bridle on the horse's head. The other end of the line was in Marsha's hand. She stayed in one spot, and the horse went around in a big circle around her, maintaining the lunge line so it was tight but not pulling. Marsha had a special lunge whip in her other hand and was simply holding it out toward the rear end of the horse. It wasn't used to actually hit him, just to keep the horse moving forward and out at the end of the line.

As I watched the lesson, I was amazed at what I saw. Marsha had the horse walking along. She told the rider to tie the end of the reins in a knot and then rest their hands on their knees. Then Marsha told the rider to hold their right arm out to the side, then their left. The horse simply continued to walk calmly along. Next, the rider held their arms out in front, then straight up in the air. Marsha told the rider to take their feet out of the stirrups and cross the stirrups in front of the saddle. "Wow," I thought, "now everything is really relying on that person's balance." I don't think I had any idea just how uncoordinated and unbalanced I truly was; all I knew was that I was feeling stronger and more confident with each passing day. I was looking forward to my lunge line lesson.

THE BALANCING ACT

My first lunge line lesson was on Apache, one of the school horses typically used for these lessons. I was so excited to brush him and get him all tacked up and ready to ride. In the tack room there were saddles, bridles, and various sizes of riding helmets to choose from. No one was ever allowed on a horse without a safety helmet on. I picked out the biggest one they had, but even that was a bit too small. I squished it down on my head and made it fit. My mom was saving up to purchase a helmet for me, so soon I would have my own.

> *"It remains a controversy, but some research does indicate a correlation between large head circumference and autism, while other research denies it. All I can say is that I had a huge head when I was a kid, and still do as an adult! Many others I know on the autism spectrum have large heads, too."*
> — *Anita Lesko*

All set to go, I then led Apache from the school barn to the indoor arena where Marsha was waiting for me. I mounted him from the mounting block and Marsha attached the lunge line through the ring on the left side of the halter, threaded it up over his head, and attached it to the other ring on the other side. That would allow her to maintain proper control of Apache at all times throughout the lesson. Apache knew his job and he walked along out on the end of the lunge line at a nice, relaxed pace. Marsha watched me in the saddle for a few minutes before starting. She wasn't much for small talk, which I appreciated. I was holding the reins as if I were riding on my own when she instructed, "Okay, go ahead and tie your reins in a knot."

It all began right there, that moment after the reins were tied in the knot and resting on the front of the saddle. I suddenly felt very vulnerable without my "crutch" of holding onto the reins. Marsha recognized that, probably from the look on my face. She simply just had Apache continue walking along for quite some time. "Stretch up tall in the saddle. You can keep your hands on your thighs, but don't reach for the reins." I did have the temptation to grab them, but I refrained from doing so. As the horse walked along, I was focusing on his movement. I slowly began to realize that something started feeling very different inside my body. It was as if my whole body was starting to wake up, starting to feel as if my arms and legs were connected, that I had purposeful movement. My hips were relaxed and swinging in synchrony with Apache's steps. It began feeling as if I was doing the walking, and his legs were mine. After a while, I no longer felt that urge to reach down and grab the reins. I started feeling perfectly fine all on my own. I started smiling, as I was enjoying the sensation throughout my body, something I had never felt before.

Marsha smiled in response to me and said, "Looks like you are having fun! That's how I want it to be. Now, I'd like you to bring your right arm out to the side and hold it there." I slowly lifted my right arm; it felt awkward and a little scary at first. After several circles like that, Marsha told me to bring my left arm out to the left, like an airplane. At first, I felt a strong urge to grab the reins. I was now relying on my body to balance itself. Marsha kept repeating, "Stretch up tall, stretch up tall," but now I felt stiff and jerky, not fluid and smooth like just moments before. "Keep trying, keep trying," I was telling myself—and I did. Marsha told me to relax and concentrate on my breathing. I started to focus on inhaling through my nose and exhaling through my mouth. I then regained my focus on Apache's footsteps, and I began to relax. As I did, I felt my hips begin swinging in synchrony again with the horse's movement. I started feeling really excited, as I realized something grand was happening.

After numerous circles, Marsha told me to rest my arms a bit. A few minutes later, she told me to hold my arms straight out in front of me, then eventually to hold them straight up in the air over my head. As I followed her instruction, the rocking sensation of my hips became more noticeable. I was still relaxed and felt very proud that I successfully did all of this. By the end of the lesson, I felt aware of my arms and legs and what they were doing.

After dismounting from Apache, it felt different with my feet now on the ground. I felt taller, with a sense of confidence I'd never had, and realized that I did have control over my body. I spent the entire day going over and over the lesson in my mind, feeling each and every step that Apache took and how my body responded to it.

By the next lunge line lesson, I felt like I had not left the saddle. This time, Marsha included dropping my feet out of the stirrups and crossing them in front of the saddle in addition to tying the reins in a knot. This was a new sensation to get used to. I was using my legs to hold on to Apache's sides. At first, I was squeezing quite hard to hold on, as he then quickened his pace, thinking I wanted him to go faster. Marsha explained that I would eventually be able to not squeeze quite so hard but instead rely on balancing myself in the saddle. She was right, that began to happen as the lesson went on. We practiced more of the same with the arms out, to the side, up in the air, but without the stirrups to steady myself on. It all was improving my balance and embedding it in my brain.

After several more lunge line lessons (and visualizing it all in my head), it all started coming together. I could sit up in the saddle with no stirrups or reins and allow my body to follow along with the movement of the horse. Soon it was second nature to me, and it all just happened without even thinking about it. I was feeling very happy and very proud of myself. I just wanted to do it more and more. I was aware of the fact that I was feeling so much better about myself, and I was starting to have more confidence in other things, like walking. I was hardly tripping any longer.

POSTING TO THE TROT: A MAJOR BREAKTHROUGH

When Marsha observed how well I was doing, she wanted to progress to more complicated activities for me to do. She wanted to start working at the trot. Fortunately, Apache had a very smooth trot, another reason they used him for the lunge line lessons. I was going to learn to post to the trot. When a horse trots, it becomes a one-two, one-two sequence, and a little faster than the walk. I was able to use the stirrups and hold the reins for this. It took a lot of coordination and a very long time to master it.

For the reader who is not familiar with posting, why it's done, and how to do it, I'll elaborate here. The trot is a particularly bumpy gait, depending on the particular horse and how he moves. I learned many years ago that warmbloods, the big European breeds like Hanoverians, Dutch, Swedish, and others, have huge trots; enough

CHAPTER 4

propulsion to make you feel like you are being tossed into the air. Of course, they are very spectacular to ride and watch when properly working through their back, on the bit, and gaits swinging freely. That's a whole book in itself!

Posting is necessary to keep you riding smoothly in the saddle during a trot, which can be a jerky stride, and also makes the movement more natural and graceful for your horse. To post, you need to lift yourself an inch or so out of the saddle by using your thigh muscles (not your feet) and your body should lean forward as well as upward. This requires being aware of the positioning of both your body and your horse's body, including proper leg positioning, steady hands and arms, and keeping your eyes ahead of you.

If you think this all sounds confusing and complicated, to a person with autism who is uncoordinated, unable to follow verbal commands, and lacks balance, it's quite a mountain to climb. Of all the techniques involved with riding a horse, this was the most difficult for me to master. It took months, and I practiced a lot at home. My dad had found an empty barrel and he built a stand to rest it on sideways to mimic a horse's back. My mom got some fabric and sewed a cushioned "saddle." Using rope and some pieces of wood, my dad fashioned stirrups. So, there in the basement, I practiced posting for hours each night. Up and down, up and down. I would visualize that I was on a horse and could really feel the trotting movement. In addition to posting at home on my barrel "horse," I spent a lot of time standing by the rail closely watching other riders posting to the trot. I was embedding that motion into my brain. It took a very long time, but I continued to do it until it became second nature to me. Of course, I wondered why it seemed so effortless for others to learn it, but I was determined nonetheless to master the posting.

Finally, I did. Each lunge line lesson got better and better, and Marsha began commenting that my balance and coordination were greatly improving. Stiffness was also an issue at first; I was very tense, which did not allow me to move smoothly. Repetition finally got me to relax. Then I was able to move with the horse in a fluid motion. I could feel the difference, and that made me really happy.

After eventually learning to post, I also learned that I could use the posting motion to adjust the horse's speed. If I sped my motion up, the horse responded by going faster; if I slowed down my movement, the horse would slow his rhythm. The process of learning to post was the turning point in truly learning to control my body. I wanted to learn it so badly that I simply wouldn't give up until it was ingrained in my mind, body, and soul. By no means did it come easily. I had to keep fighting for it. At first, my body just didn't want to cooperate with what I was telling it to do. But after visualizing it repeatedly, going through the motions on the barrel horse, and doing my lunge line lessons, it finally came together. Though the other riders simply started doing it as instructed, I never let that deter me. Instinctively, I knew I had to work a lot harder at pretty much everything, although I didn't know why. Once I learned to post, Marsha had me posting to the trot while doing the arm exercises. That helped secure my new balance and coordination.

DEVELOPING CONFIDENCE AND COORDINATION

As my coordination grew, so too did my confidence. It simply evolved without me being aware of it. Others noticed, too, and people started complimenting me on my progress. As I write this book and think back to those early days, I was quite a mess! Interestingly, no one ever said a word about my state of affairs. They were all just very patient with me. I guess they saw my struggles, and my unwavering perseverance.

Eventually, the lunge line lessons ended and I was riding on my own. By this point I had full command of the horse's body *and* my own. Marsha and the other riding instructor, Sheila, had me riding the various school horses. They wanted me to learn to ride each one, not only because their gaits were all different, but so were their personalities. The more horses I rode the more, experience I gained. The better I got, the more I wanted to do.

LEARNING TO CANTER

One day during a lesson Marsha said, "How would you like to canter today?" I was thrilled at that prospect! I'd been watching others do it and already had been visualizing it in my mind for weeks. Learning to ride the canter was challenging for me. There are a lot of steps for your body to do while the horse goes from walking to a slow, controlled gallop. We went back on the lunge line to learn to canter. Marsha thought it best for me just to focus on my body and not on the horse, too. That was fine with me.

Unlike posting, riding the canter requires you to sit deeply in the saddle, shoulders back, and following the motion of the horse with your seat. There should be no daylight between you and the saddle. A lot can go wrong with the canter, but if it's taken one step at a time, there's less chance for problems to arise. It's best to start out on the lunge line until you get the feel for the motion.

Marsha had me take hold of the front of the saddle with my two hands. She told me to sink my weight into the saddle and down through my heels. I was to sit with my shoulders back, chin up, and eyes looking straight ahead. Then, she instructed me to move my outside leg a little back behind the girth, pressing it against the horse's side. With that, the horse went from the walk into the canter. I sort of knew what to expect, but it was pretty huge! Watching other people cantering is quite different than feeling it for yourself. For whatever reason, I took to the canter like a duck to water. I didn't want to stop. That rocking-chair motion did something to me that was mesmerizing.

As time went on and I became a proficient rider, I discovered something even more grand: collection. This is the gait used in the Horse Boy Method. I learned how to sit deep in the saddle with my upper body leaning back a bit and squeeze my legs in an upward fashion. This makes a horse lower his haunches, step more deeply under himself, raise his spine, and work in a relaxed, swinging fashion. It creates a much more comfortable ride, and in gaits like collected canter, passage, piaffe, and the trot, a much bouncier sensation, more up and down, more pleasing to my senses. I just couldn't get enough of it.

Dr. Temple Grandin discusses the benefits of horseback riding in her article, "The Use of Therapy Animals with Individuals with Autism Spectrum Disorders," in the *Handbook on Animal-Assisted Therapy.* Hippotherapy is beneficial for people with ASD because it specifically addresses the vestibular system. Dr. Grandin states, "This stimulation can then lead to other benefits such as increased sensory integration ... An additional study conducted by Mason (2004) found that a therapeutic riding program tailored toward children with ASD promoted improvements in muscle tone/strength/posture, musculo-skeletal flexibility, balance/coordination, language facilitation, self-esteem, and social skills. These improvements are largely associated with the actual riding of the horse ... In a study done by Foxall (2002), it was found that the presence of the horse during therapy positively impacted the ASD person's communication skills." [XXI]

From all the physical work I was doing at the stable, my social interactions with people, and the actual riding, I was getting all the forms of horse therapy now recommended. I thought I was just having fun and enjoying myself; little did I know that every day at that stable was helping to transform me from that uncoordinated, social misfit kid to a well-functioning young adult. The process evolved over a number of years, but without that "therapy" I would not be the person I am today.

MY FIRST HORSE AND DRESSAGE

When I was older, I turned to dressage. I didn't get my first horse until I was twenty-nine, and he was a schoolmaster. He was trained to grand prix level dressage but was too old for competition. He was my teacher from whom I learned all the upper-level dressage movements. I had purchased him from a woman who was an Olympian. Once she discovered my innate ability to get any horse working through their back and on the bit, she let me ride the various horses she had in training. They were all grand prix level dressage horses. That was a real treat. It offered me more opportunities to ride collected movements. I also learned how to train a horse, eventually training a young horse through grand prix level dressage. His specialty was collected canter and passage.

When I was living in New Jersey and learning dressage, I discovered a grand place to get educated for free. The United States Equestrian Team's Olympic Training Center (USETOTC) was in Gladstone, New Jersey, about an hour away. Just prior to the 1988

Summer Olympics in Seoul, the Olympic screening trails were held at the USETOTC to select the horses/riders for the U.S. Equestrian Team, which would compete in the Olympics.

We arrived there at the crack of dawn, and for the next ten hours I sat on the bleachers of their indoor riding hall watching one Olympic hopeful after another, some already veterans of previous Olympic games, come in and ride their horses. They would first do a lengthy warmup, then get into the actual routines of their performances. Both the horses and riders were the best of the best in the world, so there I sat, "videotaping" it all in my mind. I was recording every last detail of each and every one of them. What was most obvious was their dedication, determination, and demand for perfection of both themselves and their mount.

Mom and I stayed in a nearby hotel and I went again the next day to watch again. Once back home, I re-played all my video footage in my brain for weeks. I visualized myself doing all of those things on my own horse. To this day, I can still see each of those riders putting their horses through the paces: how they sat in the saddle, each tiny shift of their weight, how they held the reins, what their legs were doing, everything. I remember details that others would never notice, changes that are for the most part imperceptible to the naked eye. In fact, when you watch Olympic-level dressage riders, it appears that each top-hat and tails rider is just sitting pretty atop their magnificent horse, who is performing spectacularly all by herself. I absorbed all of it and actually visualized it for many years following that experience.

CHAPTER 4

THINKING LIKE A HORSE

The more I was around horses and studied their behavior, the more I realized we were very much alike. Despite not knowing I'm on the autism spectrum, I did know I had numerous characteristics that others didn't seem to share. I had a feel for each horse, sort of an innate sensitivity and intuition about them. Not everyone has this ability; I felt lucky that I could perceive exactly what they were feeling. I always had anxiety, even on a good day. It wouldn't take much to instantly increase the level. When I was around the horses, though, my anxiety dramatically decreased. I observed that horses also displayed anxiety. It could easily be seen if something scared them or they perceived imminent danger. They'd suddenly lift their head up, ears forward, whites of their eyes showing. That is their natural flight or fight response. This fear can result in a potentially dangerous reaction. World famous horse trainer Linda Tellington-Jones discusses the significance of this in her book, *The Ultimate Horse Behavior and Training Book*, and the possibility of looking for a different horse if you feel nervous around a particular horse. It is not worth getting seriously injured.

HORSES HAVE MELTDOWNS, JUST LIKE INDIVIDUALS WITH AUTISM

I learned early on to trust my instincts. I could also see that horses get stressed for many reasons. If the stress continued, they'd have a "meltdown," just like me. One instance that clearly stands out in my head was at a dressage clinic I was attending as an audience member. I was thrilled to have front row seats. The trainer was working with the rider to start the beginning steps of piaffe: a highly collected movement in which you train the horse to trot in place, to lower his haunches, bring up his back, and rhythmically trot on the spot. It is a very advanced stage of learning, which one builds up to over several years. To do it safely and correctly, it is taught very slowly and in stages while giving regular praise and breaks for relaxation. To push a horse will result in exactly what I witnessed that day.

It just so happened that the horse, rider, and trainer ended up stopping right in front of me to work on the piaffe. The trainer kept telling the rider to sit deeper in the saddle, leaning their weight back a little, and continue squeezing with their legs while restraining the horse from moving forward. The horse started getting stressed. I could see it on his face. The trainer had a long whip in her hand, the kind used in dressage for this kind of work. She started reaching under the horse with it and tapping the back of the horse's legs. She was trying to convey to him to pick up each hoof, but the horse was getting sensory overload at that point. He started swishing his tail and snorting. He also broke out in a foaming sweat. As I looked on, I couldn't believe what I was seeing. I wondered how the rider or trainer couldn't recognize they were pushing that horse beyond his limit. The horse had massive stimuli to cope with: he was being ridden in front of thousands of people, the instructor was wearing a headset to amplify what she was saying, he was being asked to do something new with a whip tapping his legs, and was receiving multiple signals from the rider. It all built up. I saw it coming. Suddenly, the horse erupted into a frenzied explosion, kicking out his hind legs violently and rearing straight up. The rider managed to stay on. Those in the front row, including myself, just missed getting hit with flying hooves. That's how I experience a meltdown, with stimuli building up inside of me until the eruption. (I don't kick out or rear up, just for the record!) I simply couldn't understand why no one else saw that coming. They seemed quite shocked that it happened. Over

CHAPTER 4

the years I saw people who had a great horse, even Olympic-caliber horses, who pushed the horse too hard and too fast and literally gave the animal a nervous breakdown. Once that happens, that's pretty much the end of that horse's career. It would take years to undo that mental stress, if ever.

HIGH ANXIETY

I also learned how to deal with my high anxiety, something that has affected me since I was a child, and actually still does to this day. I'm not sure how old I was at the time, probably around six or seven when it started. One night, I was already in bed when I heard my mom crying downstairs. I started listening carefully, as she and my dad were talking. I couldn't quite make out what they were saying, so I cautiously got out of bed and tiptoed over to the stairwell where I could hear much better. From what I was hearing, mom was crying about financial issues, that she was so worried we were going to lose everything. The more I heard the more scared I got. That was quite a burden for a little kid to hear. From then on, I always felt worried and sick inside. It made me even more dependent on my mom to make me feel secure. Indeed, we *were* poor. Mom sewed all my clothes, all food was made from scratch, and we only had one vehicle, which was always some cheap jalopy my dad would find. He was always working under the hood fixing something to keep it running. One vehicle was so pathetic, he needed to put door hinges on the car doors to prevent them from falling off. The hinges were visible from the outside. It was a teeny tiny, two-tone Metropolitan. Yellow on the top and white on the bottom. He'd joke about it looking like a lemon, as it truly was a lemon. He also built most of the furniture we had from scrap wood he'd find.

BECOMING AN AUTISM SUCCESS STORY

Mom would sew seat cushions for the chairs and paint them. They were primitive, but served their purpose. I didn't realize how poor we were until the time mom started cleaning houses to earn money, and sometimes I'd go with her to help. It was then where I saw how other people lived, quite differently than us. That made my anxiety get even worse.

I can now realize why my obsession with horses often made my mom sad. When I'd start crying because I so badly wanted my own horse, she would start crying too, trying to explain that it was very expensive to buy and maintain a horse. All I knew was that I wanted a horse, and that was all I could focus on.

Once I became a working student at the stable, I would learn that horses get anxiety, too. There were so many things about their behavior that I identified with.

ALL HORSES HAVE ASPERGER'S

There was a stable hand who, to me back then, seemed like a thousand years old. He worked in the main barn where the privately-owned horses were stabled. I only knew his first name, Moe. I quickly recognized that he had a very special connection to all the horses. He was very laid back and extremely quiet. He rarely said a word. There was always a piece of straw sticking out the side of his mouth that he chewed on. His job was cleaning stalls, feeding, watering, and taking horses out to the paddock then bring them back in. I was fascinated watching him around the horses. He had an overwhelming sense of calmness about him, and it had the same effect on the horses.

Though I typically had anxiety, being around the horses gave me extreme peace and comfort. I observed that if I did have anxiety, the horse I was with sensed it and he too became anxious. They were like a mirror of my emotions. You cannot fool a horse. They can sense whatever emotion you are experiencing. This is another excellent reason that horses are used for therapy, because of the fact that they are mirrors of your emotions. It helps the person recognize what they are feeling, and how to redirect their emotions.

The stable was located pretty much right in a neighborhood, such that there were homes on either side of the entire facility, but the entire back of the place was adjacent to a 408-acre reservation. There were gorgeous trails to ride through the woods there, but in order to get actually to the reservation you had to ride under the main road through a tunnel. There was a stream which ran through it, only about six to eight inches deep. One of the reasons I wasn't much interested in going on a trail ride was that you had to go through that tunnel to get to the trails. I felt uneasy the few times I did go. The tunnel was basically a bridge over the stream for the roadway above. It was a very busy county road, so when you were down in the tunnel, an echo from all the vehicles passing overhead was readily audible.

I had heard that it was scary going through there; often, horses were afraid to attempt it and would spin around and start galloping back to the barn. One day, we all decided to be adventurous and go on a trail ride. Several of the working students and myself set out on this big event. Our instructor led the way, and we all followed her in single file. We went through a brief area of woods then emerged out into the open field. We could see the highway, with cars and semis zipping along. There was a well-worn path that was obvious, leading down to the tunnel. The pitch was great enough that the horses instinctively lowered their heads and necks and stepped cautiously on the dirt and crumbled rocks. Occasionally, I'd feel a hoof slip out from under Popcorn, the horse I was riding. Marsha had called out to all of us to lean our weight backward a little to reduce the chance of the horse stumbling enough to fall. As the entrance to the tunnel came into sight, I got very concerned. It looked like a black hole. I knew in that instant the horses weren't going to be happy about walking into darkness.

Marsha had been there many times on the horse she was riding. That was the only saving grace. Her horse readily began walking into the tunnel and into the water. I was right behind her. Fortunately, horses like to follow the horse in front of them. As my turn loomed closer to step into the darkness, Popcorn started coiling up under me and put her brakes on, coming to a screeching halt. She was starting to turn around, telling me she wasn't going in there. She was turning to the right, so I pulled my left rein to pull her head back towards the tunnel and began squeezing hard with both legs. She finally sensed my can-do attitude and reluctantly began her journey under the bridge. When her first leg felt the water, she leaped a few steps then settled down to walk normally. Once in the tunnel, we could see the daylight at the other end. It was actually a thrilling experience as we continued through the stream with the water running past us. Popcorn was relaxed as we made our way through and out into the bright sunlight. She wanted to canter up the hill, so I let her, getting up out of the saddle and forward, allowing her hind legs to power us up the steep incline. Marsha was waiting at the top on the level surface. What an experience!

MY ROUTINES

As the summer went on, I spent most of my time downstairs where all the school horses were stalled. In the early mornings when I first would arrive at the stable, I had a routine that I started. I loved routines, as they gave me a sense of comfort, security, and order. I loved the aroma of fresh shavings. It was an earthy smell that was like perfume to me. I would walk around the entire place, stopping at each horse's stall. I went around in the same exact pattern each day, and the horses soon came to expect to see me. If anything was out of its usual place, I would instantly notice it, wondering why it wasn't where it was supposed to be. I soon observed that horses also loved routines, and they, too, would notice any little thing that was moved, or anything new in their environment.

I would hold the bars on the stall and peer through them at the occupant inside. It was early morning, just at dawn. As I walked into the building, I would savor the pastel colors of the morning sunrise. Birds would be singing and flying around in the high ceiling. Most of the horses were already standing near their feed buckets, waiting for breakfast to arrive. As I looked at each horse, they would come over to sniff at me, blowing softly through their nostrils as they investigated me. I could feel the tickle of their whiskers on my face as they pressed their nose against the bars. I would look deeply into their big, beautiful eyes. I wondered why I could look into a horse's eyes forever, yet it actually felt painful to look into the eyes of a human. I avoided that at all cost. Of course, I didn't know this was a symptom of Asperger's syndrome.

I was in my own little world, simply focused on savoring every moment at the barn. My dad would drop me off at the barn at dawn each day on his way to work, and I'd be there until five o'clock in the evening. My dad worked just up the road from the stable, so it worked out really well. Back in those days, there were no such thing as cell phones, just old-fashioned phones attached to walls in public places. There was one such phone, a pay-phone, on the wall in the main barn. It would cost twenty-five cents to make a local call. We couldn't afford to pay for all the calls I made to mom all day, so we had a system: I'd put in my quarter, dial our house, and let it ring twice. That was the signal it was me calling. Then I'd hang up, my quarter would drop back down to retrieve, and mom would then call me back. If she needed to get hold of me, she could also simply call that number, and someone would answer it. Everyone there knew me, so they could quickly locate me to tell me to call home. I would call her the second I arrived there to let her know I arrived safely. Then I was on to making my rounds of all my horse friends. Throughout the day I'd make many calls home, to let Mom know I was okay (and sometimes just for emotional support).

HELICOPTER PARENTS

Prior to my passion for horses, I was plastered to my mom. It was the magnetic force of the horses which got me on track for starting to develop independence from my mom and being home. When I first became a working student, she accompanied me to the barn and would sit in the lounge all day, equipped with numerous books to read. She wanted to be close by in case something happened to me and to be sure I'd be safe. Eventually, she would just come for horse shows or other special occasions. She never really got to do any reading, as the other working student kids sort of adopted her and would sit with her, telling her all their woes. My nickname was "Bone," so she was "Ma Bone." I guess I might have to admit my mom was a helicopter mom in some respects, but I put limits on that. Looking back, I was a pretty obnoxious kid.

I don't want to offend anyone, but I feel the need to talk about "helicopter parenting," especially in regard to mothers. Being a helicopter parent is defined as "being involved in a child's life in a way that is overcontrolling, overprotecting, and over perfecting, in a way that is in excess of responsible parenting." XXII In the case of children on the autism spectrum, it is very normal for any parent to become a helicopter parent. Children (and adults) on the spectrum can be very naïve about others and the ways of the world, uncoordinated, and have numerous other areas that necessitate much more intense, watchful, and involved parenting. In fact, I'd say that we all need helicopter parents. This does, however, require a balancing act. The parent needs to, at some point, allow the child to begin gaining their own independence. That is something the parent needs to gauge themselves, as it will be different for each child—and it will certainly be different than a neurotypical child.

I always hear parents of children with autism talking about their fears for their child's future. They worry about how their child will fend for themselves once they, the parents, are gone. That's a great question, and that's exactly why they need to be pro-active in helping their child gain independence. There's a great book by Dr. Temple Grandin to help with this specific issue: *The Loving Push: How Parents and Professionals Can Help Spectrum Kids Become Successful Adults.*

Back when I was a kid, aside from the fact that we didn't know I was on the autism spectrum, there were no books on this topic. My mom recognized I was different and needed intense guidance and close supervision, and so the hovering began. I loved every minute of it. She always made me feel secure and comforted. I felt extremely insecure when I had to be away from her, like when I had to start attending kindergarten. The elementary school I attended was in my hometown of Bloomfield, New Jersey. Each morning, my mom walked me to school, and brought me right up to the door of my classroom. I felt sick to my stomach to let go of her hand. The only comfort I had was knowing where she was going next. If you were in the kindergarten classroom, you could see out the window to a tree with a bench under it. The distance from the window was probably about 800 feet away. She'd walk over to that bench and sit there until it was time to get me after class was over. I could see her out the window all day, which made me feel secure. (Yes, I was a mess. Other than my husband, Abraham, I've never shared this with anyone.)

Of course, the school administration was berserk that she did this, but the bench wasn't on school property, so they couldn't chase her away. They kept calling her in to say it was really bad for me that she continued to sit there each day. She simply wasn't about to leave me there. Our bond was too strong. I didn't know any better, I just knew that I was terrified to be away from her.

That is, until I got involved with horses. Horses have a way of making you feel empowered. Horses have the innate capacity to awaken, heal, and empower the human spirit. I truly believe there is a connection between humans, nature, and horses. The best medicine on earth can be a horse.

I was so focused on everything at the barn that I didn't give a thought about being away from Mom. It all happened naturally and evolved over time. Once I walked through those stable doors each morning, I was thinking about all I had to get done. It so vital in helping me to gain my independence.

As the weeks went on, I started taking on more responsibility. I'm not quite sure how it all came about, but I just got in there and did stuff. I was pretty pushy. Maybe you'd call it assertive...but probably pushy. The more responsibilities I took on, the higher my self-confidence grew. I started feeling much better about myself, and a sense of pride began to emerge. All of that started spilling over into my life outside of the stable, and others began to notice it about me.

Working around the school horses, cleaning stalls, and feeding wasn't enough for me. I wanted to be in charge of everything. There were people who worked there that were getting paid, but they were more than happy to rest when I began running the show. I started taking charge of the lesson horses, so I'd look at the schedule to see which horses were supposed to go out at what time. I'd then brush each one and have them tacked up and ready to go for their riders. Keeping track of those going out and those coming back from lessons became a real-life merry-go-round. Often, the horses were hot and sweating and needed to be walked and cooled out. Most of the time I'd walk them. If I had too much going on, I'd delegate the task to another working student. Somehow, I just took charge. No one said otherwise, so I simply continued doing what I was doing. When there was a lull in the lesson schedule, I'd start cleaning all the saddles and bridles in the tack room. I'd put a saddle rack near the doorway, so I could look outside as I cleaned the saddles. I loved the feel of the leather, the smell, the tiny tack sponge, and the texture of the glycerin saddle soap used to clean the tack.

To me, this was heaven. The reality was that it was serving multiple purposes for me. Indeed, it was allowing me to gain my independence. Beyond that, I was learning how to work, how to interact with people, and developing management skills. It was providing me the very things that books, conferences, and therapists are recommending today for people on the autism spectrum who are transitioning into adulthood. My friend, Temple Grandin, and I have talked extensively about this very issue. Temple had the same experiences working in a stable in boarding school. Often, kids today just aren't getting any kind of work experience, so when they graduate from high school and it's time to go to college or get a job, they're lost. They have zero skills. There shouldn't need to be a specific transition, as it should have occurred gradually over time. When it occurs gradually, you are more inclined to remember everything you are learning and build upon all the skills you are developing.

I highly encourage parents to get their kids involved in household chores, and to get out in the world volunteering or working. The earlier they start, the easier their life will be later on when it's time to either go to college, a trade school, or seek employment. I'm pushing for kids to get involved with horses because of the many different facets this has for the individual with autism, but there are so many options out there, perhaps involving your child's special interest, that can provide practical life experience and important lessons. I just so happen to believe that in the transformative powers of horses and the human-animal connection.

HOW CHILDHOOD JOBS PREPARED ME FOR SUCCESS AS AN ADULT WITH AUTISM

(Adapted from an article written for The Mighty.) [XXIII]

I have the good fortune to be a friend of Dr. Temple Grandin. We have a lot in common. We both have autism, and we share a very similar youth that played a big factor in our adult life. We both started jobs at a very early age. Temple often talks about her early days, when her job was to greet guests at the door for her mom's dinner party and take their coats to hang up. Yes, it was a job. She was given a responsibility to carry out.

Among her numerous other childhood jobs was the one I, too, did for many years—mucking out horse stalls. In many conversations with Temple, we've talked about those days of our teenage years spent shoveling out one stall after another. We both love horses and being around them. It was peaceful, and it was also a form of therapy. In essence, it was our occupational therapy.

All of the childhood jobs we did prepared us for the day when we'd start our careers. We were used to working, showing up on time, following orders from a boss, figuring out how to get a job done. It was just a regular part of our life. So, when the day came to embark into our careers, we really didn't have to transition into anything. We were already there.

Temple is world-famous for her life and career. She's beyond amazing! She inspires everyone, whether they are on the spectrum or not. I also hope to inspire people with my story and wisdom. I've got a lot to offer.

Statistics show that 85 percent of people on the autism spectrum are unemployed or underemployed. That's a staggering number. I see this to be a very complex situation with multiple factors. One of those factors can be changed by parents. Get your kid working! Every little chore you have them do around the house is a job. Having them help you set the table, do laundry, tidy up; it's all working. Once they become a teenager, jobs that have more responsibility are in order. Cutting lawns in the neighborhood, helping elderly neighbors, or working at a fast-food restaurant can build the foundation for a child's future in the workforce. It also exposes them to many different things, one of which might strike their fancy enough to make a career out of it!

HOME CHORES

I can't remember a time when I wasn't working. As a young kid, my mom would have me helping her in the kitchen. She'd teach me the art of cooking and baking, and under her close supervision she would give me little jobs to carry out. I would be "assigned" to gather all the ingredients for baking a cake. After I'd assemble everything on the counter, she would stand by me as I followed the recipe and mixed up the batter. Of course, safety was always her first concern, so she would use the mixer until I was old enough to be able to safely handle it. Then I'd get to pour the batter into the pan, mom would put it into the oven, she'd take it out, and once cool, I'd put the icing on the cake. I would feel very proud of my accomplishment! I'd be chattering away to her during that whole time, as she was my best friend.

WORKING AT THE STABLE

I fell in love with horses around the age of two. It became one of my special interests, one that has sustained my entire life. I desperately wanted to learn to ride. Unfortunately, my parents were unable to afford riding lessons for me. When I was twelve, I became a working student at a nearby stable. In return for work, you could earn riding lessons. I became quite proficient at mucking out stalls. The more I shoveled, the more riding time I got. I dreamed of jumping horses over big fences in competition. My dream eventually came true, because by the time I was sixteen, I was jumping horses over six-foot-high fences in some pretty big shows. It was my hard work, perseverance, and visualization that got me there.

During all those summers and weekends spent at the stable, I not only mucked out stalls and did other tasks like painting fences, picking rocks out of pastures, emptying trash bins, etc. I was interacting with people, learning to follow orders, knowing the importance of showing up on time, getting a job done, and feeling pride in myself. Little did I know that all of those things were preparing mc for my "real" job.

Besides the stable job, once in college I held a variety of other great jobs. I worked as a graphic arts designer at my undergraduate college for the four years I was there. That was with their working student program, which deducted the money I would have earned from my tuition. I also worked as a skate guard at a public ice-skating arena. It was my first job that I actually received a paycheck for! I was into ice dancing for a number of years, and because I worked at the arena, it allowed me to get free ice time for practicing. That job also entailed selling tickets at the window for the public skating sessions, making popcorn and hot dogs in the snack shop, and other sundry tasks. Again, these jobs were preparing me for my future. Because I had already developed the work skills at the stable, I was easily able to take on new jobs. The jobs at the ice arena were, however, more challenging. At the stable I didn't have to interact with people too much. Some, but nowhere near what I had to do at the arena: interacting with people was at least 60 percent of the job. During concerts, ice shows, and the various other events they held there, you would mostly find me at the food concession! I enjoyed making cotton candy, hot dogs, popcorn, and other such festive eats. Then came the fun part: taking orders from each customer, getting them what they wanted, then ringing up everything on the old-fashioned cash register. In those days, it was basically an adding machine. It didn't tell me how much change they should receive. I had to figure it out in my head, or at worst case scenario, I always had a notepad and pencil to figure it out on paper. Also, there was no such thing as swiping a card to process an order! For the young people reading this, it is probably hard to imagine the antiquated cash register. At first, it nearly sent me into a meltdown. There were dozens of customers in line, bright lights, announcements constantly going on, music playing, multiple conversations all around me, and various aromas from the food being prepared. Each of my senses was getting overloaded. I figured out how to narrow my focus to only what I was actually needing to do. Yet in addition, I had to look at each customer to take their order, and look them in the eye! I was very thankful for all those endless trips to the mall with my mom, and visualizing how to look people in the eye. Each and every interaction just continued to set the foundation for my future success. I'm sure there were plenty of blunders I made, and sometimes I'd notice someone roll their eyes, yet I kept going. I sensed that the more I interacted with people, the easier it got for me, and the more comfortable I got doing it.

OPERATING SPOTLIGHTS

Another thing I dreamed to do was operating the spotlights for various shows. The spotlights were located way up high in the center of the ceiling of the arena. The only access to get up there was a narrow ladder, which was affixed to the curved dome of the building. It wasn't for the faint of heart. I had to do a lot of pestering to be able to finally do it, and I simply never gave up on that until the boss conceded. I watched the guys who operated the lights many times. Once I was finally up there, I again watched them. Then I just got right up in there and began doing it. Of course, I had on a safety harness hooked up to the railing, and also a headset to be able to take directions from the stage manager. I learned that very quickly and became a regular at it. The worst part was the first time I had to come back down from way up there! I looked down and sort of panicked! I came down very slowly, backward.

DRIVING A ZAMBONI

If you've ever been to a skating arena you probably know what a Zamboni machine is. They use it to resurface the ice. I desperately wanted to drive that thing. It took a long time and my famous pestering to get on it, but eventually I got them to cave! Meanwhile, I spent much time studying the Zamboni being operated, over and over and over. I took mental notes of the speed, when they would ease up to be able to make the corners without skidding into the side walls, every last detail. So when I finally got to drive it, I knew what to do. The guys who drove it were baffled as to how I did so well. I told them how I visualized it over and over in my mind. They were pretty freaked out.

BAKING BUSINESS

While I was in undergraduate school, I ran a cake baking business for about two years. It started when I baked a very decadent cake for a lady friend of my mom. The lady's husband was a very successful businessman, with clientele accordingly. They saw and tasted that cake and began putting in orders for more. Our kitchen was always a mess, flour everywhere, as I would be baking and decorating the cakes in between studying for my courses. It was lots of fun, and yet another job that I learned a lot from while I did it, like interacting with more people.

This, of course, shows the extreme importance of getting out there and doing stuff! Whether it is a volunteer job, a paid job, or work in return for something (like riding lessons), it is getting you ready for success in your future.

VOLUNTEERING AT A LOCAL HOSPITAL LED TO MY CAREER

Oh yes, let me tell you how my career found me! When I used to be into ice dancing, one day while practicing I fell and fractured my left arm. I ended up at the hospital emergency department. While I was there waiting for the orthopedic surgeon to arrive to set and cast my arm, the anesthesiologist was talking to me. He asked what I do, to which I replied, "I'm going to college to become a nurse." He then inquired, "Why don't you go to be a nurse anesthetist?" Having never heard of that, I asked him what a nurse anesthetist is. He told me that it's a nurse who first gets a bachelor of science in nursing, of which I was already in my fourth year. Then you need at least two years of critical care experience in an intensive care unit, or some similar experience. Then it's a two-year master's program of extremely intense study and clinical experience in the operating room doing anesthesia. Once graduated and board-certified, you work in the operating room doing anesthesia for all different kinds of surgery. And you can even choose a particular specialty if you'd like.

It was that moment, sitting there on a stretcher in an exam room of the ER, with my fractured arm, that my career as a nurse anesthetist was born! I was instantly intrigued. So, after that, I set sail to embark on the new journey. After graduating from Bloomfield College with my BSN, I started working in a very busy emergency department at a big hospital. I also had to go two more years to earn all the courses required to apply to the nurse anesthesia program at Columbia University. It was basically pre-med courses: two years of biology, one year general chemistry, one year organic chemistry, one year of physics, and one year microbiology. It wasn't easy taking all that while working full time. I then applied to Columbia University and waited for the reply. At the time I went there, theirs was the second-highest accredited program in the country, with Stanford's being the first. I was accepted, and so it all began. Had I not fallen and broke my arm, I wouldn't have met that anesthesiologist who suggested becoming a CRNA. See the importance of getting out there and doing stuff? You never know what you will discover you are interested in doing unless you try many things. The more things you get involved in, the more likely you will find a new path in life.

In 1988, I graduated from Columbia University in New York City with my master of science in nurse anesthesia and embarked on my (currently) thirty-year career as a certified registered nurse anesthetist. I've been working full time ever since, in a job that's not for the faint of heart. The operating room is a very fast-paced, ever-changing, high-stress environment, loaded with massive sensory violations. Most significantly, as I call it, I'm floating in an ocean of neurotypicals! I would have sunk long ago without all the life experiences of those jobs I'd done in my younger days. I would not have been prepared to interact with people, situations, and the job itself. To date I've done over 60,000 anesthetics, and as I've carefully calculated, I've interacted with over one million people. That's a lot, particularly for a person with autism.

My specialty area in anesthesia is neuroanesthesia, which is anesthesia for neurosurgery cases like aneurysm clippings, brain tumors, spinal fusions, and more. It's highly detailed and complex, just what a person on the autism spectrum loves. I did that for many years. I also specialized in anesthesia for organ transplants/trauma/burns. Now I enjoy working with a great team of very busy orthopedic surgeons doing anesthesia and spinals for total joint replacement surgery.

When I see articles about transitioning from school to work, I wonder why the transition is always such a big deal. I believe work experience should start early and be part of education. Working a job and all that comes with it should be second nature by the time students graduate. If it isn't, life will be very stressful, and possibly even unsuccessful. Those 85 percent of us who are unemployed or underemployed might have had a different story if they were prepared to enter the job market. If you have never worked any kind of job as a kid and teenager, nothing can substitute for that lack of life skills. The job market is highly competitive for everyone, even neurotypicals. For those on the autism spectrum, it's far more difficult. But it's up to parents to get your kids out there doing various jobs at an early age. Start them at home doing chores. Something. Anything. Always, however, be sure of the child's safety.

Having autism and working a career-type job is like going to a foreign country, not speaking their language, and trying to survive. To this day, all these years later, I still feel like a foreigner in a strange land. Yet I've built enough experience and "learned the language" enough to have a successful career. I know without a doubt in my mind that I would never have made it as an anesthetist if I hadn't had all my previous jobs.

I hope every parent will recognize the importance of teaching their child the skills to succeed at work. Keeping them sheltered is not helpful and can set them up for failure. The only way to get skilled at socializing, learn responsibility, and learn to work is by getting out there and doing it. The more an individual with autism interacts with others, the better they get at it. Therapists, counselors, and the like all have their places in helping those on the autism spectrum, but nothing can substitute for real-life experiences. Nothing.

Upon completion of school, going out and seeking a job shouldn't be a first-time experience. Having to learn a new job is stressful enough. If you are prepared ahead of time with years of life experience, you will be able to use all your energy to focus on the job. If you are also having to learn how to interact with people, how to follow orders, and how to get along in the workplace, it may seem insurmountable, and you're basically setting yourself up for failure.

I believe it is a parent's duty to help prepare their child with autism for the future by giving them chores, then in their teen years getting them out there doing some type of job. Real-life experience can only be learned by first-hand experience. Sure, your kid will make blunders.

I've made plenty, and still do! But I keep going. And they will too. It will be the best "therapy" you can ever give your child. Help them to have a job and be able to support themselves for the rest of their life.

CHAPTER 5

PERSONAL SUCCESSES

"The biggest adventure you can take is to live the life of your dreams."

– OPRAH WINFREY

CHAPTER 5

Earlier, I discussed how I used visualization to learn to ride horses. As time went on and I encountered new challenges, I continued to use visualization in pretty much everything else. Because I didn't discover that I'm on the autism spectrum until later in life, I didn't understand why I was so different and never fit in. I didn't spend too much time dwelling on that. Instead, I was always forging ahead and following my passion for my next adventure! With that said, I will add that for everything I've ever tackled, visualization and changing my brain through neuroplasticity came into play. I use visualization even for things that seem small, like preparing to go into a new store or restaurant for the first time. I need to visualize the front entrance, how it will feel to walk in there, and what to expect once inside. If I can pull up the website for the establishment, I'll do that, too, so I can see what it's like inside. That helps with my visualization. To some it may sound silly to have to do this before going somewhere for the first time, but it dramatically decreases my anxiety over it as I then feel as if I have already been there before. Once you get comfortable with visualizing, you will turn to it for most everything you do. It will become second nature to you.

SOCIAL SKILLS

This is a biggie for a person with autism. Despite the fact that we were poor, my mom and I used to go to the mall on Saturday mornings and just wander through stores. We couldn't afford to buy anything, but just getting out, seeing new things, and people-watching was fun. Our favorite thing to do was get a coffee and sit at the edge of the food court at lunchtime. There were hundreds of people, probably more, coming to eat with their friends and families. We would simply sit there, watching everyone and commenting on their facial expressions and body movements. We were always extremely fascinated at how different they all were from us. I would watch one after another, studying how they made endless facial expressions as they talked and interacted with others. It was like being in a foreign country. No matter how many times I saw facial expressions, I thought it looked ridiculous and, often, over exaggerated. I saw absolutely no point in this activity, and neither one of us could figure out why everyone did this. What I did take to heart was how people moved their bodies while interacting with others. I studied this over and over. I recognized it, too, was quite different than what I would do. I instinctively knew I should conduct myself more in the manner that everyone else was.

LEARNING TO MAKE EYE CONTACT

The other thing I observed was that people would look directly into one another's eyes. Ouch. It was actually painful to even watch this, let alone do it myself, but obviously this was what I was supposed to do. Despite that I was beginning to talk a little more readily to others, to look at them in their eyes made me feel ill at ease, almost reaching a feeling of hysteria inside. It made me feel like I wanted to run away from the person. I also recognized just how uncomfortable I made others from my reactions to them.

Eye contact was one of the more difficult tasks I've undertaken, and I still have difficulty with it. I thought and thought. How could I start doing this? Multiple times a day, for about ten minutes at a time, I started visualizing looking into people's eyes. At first, I'd envision people that I knew and visualize looking directly into their eyes. Even though I wasn't actually doing it, I felt horribly uncomfortable, just as if I were doing it for real. Of course, I expected this to happen, I knew that this wasn't going to be easy. That's why I stuck to short periods multiple times a day, and worked at it for an entire month. This was extremely difficult. I didn't know why it was so difficult, but that didn't matter. What did matter was that I was forging ahead, persevering, and maintaining patience. To liven things up, I started to visualize looking into the eyes of strangers. At the mall, I'd randomly pick out people and visualize looking into their eyes. I focused on keeping myself relaxed during these short sessions. Finally, getting into week four, it began feeling more natural. I started to feel like it was no big deal to look into anyone's eyes, whether it was someone I knew or a complete stranger.

I was ready to test out my new skill. One after another, everyone I had to talk to, I was able to look them in the eye as I interacted with them. I discovered that people seemed more relaxed talking to me, or maybe I was more relaxed. The conversations seemed to go much more smoothly, and people didn't appear to want to get away from me like before. It was truly a struggle to get through that month of "training," but it seemed to be making all the difference in the world.

I would seek out every opportunity possible to make small talk with people. The more I did it, the easier it became. I also studied people at the mall as to how they looked into other's eyes. Obviously, there's a big difference in this depending on who you're talking to: how I look into my husband's eyes is very different than how I look at someone standing by the bell peppers in the grocery store. When I look into my husband's eyes I look deeply, with a feeling like I'm looking into his soul. As for the stranger in the store, it's a casual look at them, and not for too long. It's perfectly okay to look at someone in the eyes, glance away for a moment, then look back at them. Even neurotypicals do that. Once I was totally comfortable with that, I became able to maintain direct eye contact during conversations. Through my visualization, I rewired my brain to do something that was totally unnatural to me as a person with autism, yet now it was second nature. This new skill would later be very helpful for the rest of my life.

VISUALIZING BODY LANGUAGE

After having eye contact mastered, I moved on to body movements. Of course, now I know it's properly called "body language," but then I just thought it was odd ways people acted when talking to others. I tend to make a lot of hand movements when I talk. I'm not sure if that's where I picked it up from, but I've been like that my whole life. When I first saw Temple Grandin talking, I noticed she is also very active with her hands. Maybe it's an autism thing. In any case, that has stayed with me my whole life.

I thought I might be able to make the same kinds of movements neurotypicals do when talking, so I began visualizing them. I'd envision watching myself making these movements. That went on for years—not weeks, not months, but years! It felt completely unnatural and fake to me. I saw no need for making exaggerated facial expressions or body movements then, and in fact, I still really don't!

I never pretended to be someone else or to be "normal." I didn't even know how to try to be "normal," as I didn't know I had autism in the first place! I did, however, recognize that other people seemed to have more successful social interactions than I did, which spurred me into paying close attention to their facial expressions and movements to try to figure how their system worked.

CHAPTER 5

Social skills were probably the hardest things I've ever challenged myself to learn, because they made no sense to me. I thought the neurotypicals thought like I did. Ultimately, I found out I was wrong.

Regarding social skills, yes, visualization is extremely important to use to improve yourself. However, the bottom line is that you must get out there and interact with others to achieve success—and not just with others on the spectrum. *Everyone.* I am a very big fan of any school which promotes inclusion of children on the spectrum with neurotypical children. They will learn from each other. It's no different concerning adults on the spectrum. You can't stay home until you are eighteen or twenty, sitting in the basement playing video games, then suddenly expect to go to college or get a job. If you have zero experience working or interacting with others, it is going to be markedly more difficult for you to succeed. Transition programs are helpful, but nothing will get you better suited for life than real-life experience, and lots of it. When people say to me, "Oh! You are so lucky you have mastered social skills and can talk and act like anyone else," I think of a quote by Thomas Jefferson: "The harder you work, the luckier you get." What people see today is the culmination of a lifetime of non-stop work!

NAVIGATING COLLEGE WITH VISUALIZATION

When I was going to start college, it was in my hometown of Bloomfield, New Jersey. It was a small college, but to me it was overwhelming at first. The buildings were spread out over several blocks, so the first thing I did was request a map of the campus. I studied that until I knew it in extreme detail. I went to the campus weeks before classes started to walk around and physically see where each building was, and actually went inside and looked for the exact room numbers where my classes would be. If the room was unoccupied, I would go in it and look around. I'd do this several times. I would even pick out which seat I wanted to sit in and go sit in it. I typically always sat right in the front row, positioning myself to be closest to the instructor. I recognized very early on that if I sat right there in the front row, I would have minimal sensory input from all the other students. If you sit anywhere else in the room, you can then see everyone, and easily become distracted from all of them squirming in their seats or talking to others. I did this enough times that I knew exactly where to go for each class, and feel comfortable, like I've been there many times. This helped to calm me down.

The next step was getting the syllabus for each glass and "mapping" out each class for the whole semester. Using a huge calendar, I'd plot out all my assignments on the dates they were due. Essay papers, exams, or anything special would go on that calendar. This made it very easy for me to look at the months and visualize which assignments were due and when. Then I would narrow that down by making lists of things that were due in the immediate future. All details concerning these things would be included; for example, let's say that at the end of the second week there was a test and a short paper due. I'd write down what needs to be read to prepare for the test, and what the paper should be about. Then, going yet another step, I'd write down *when* I needed to do those things. I made a little box next to each item so that and check it off when it was done to keep myself organized.

This routine helped me remain organized at all times. Of course, there were other things I would have to include on my master calendar, such as my work schedule. I learned very quickly that literally every minute counted, so I planned ahead to use my free time to study and prepare for the next task. Feeling organized and visualizing ahead dramatically decreased my anxiety.

Throughout my four years earning my bachelor of science in nursing, I worked three different jobs, totaling about twenty hours a week. I took out over $100,000 in student loans for undergraduate and graduate school, but that still didn't cover everything, so I made up the money working. I paid back all my student loans over a ten-year span after I graduated.

ANESTHESIA TRAINING

When I was working on my master's at Columbia University to become a certified registered nurse anesthetist, it was an overwhelming experience. There were only six students in the anesthesia program as the school purposefully kept as a small class. Being the different one who didn't fit in, I was always the outsider, which added more stress on top of the intense course load and training in the operating room. I know that many times the instructors were ready to pull their hair out over me.

The operating room is a daunting and sacred place. There is a patient on the operating table whose very life is dependent on the anesthesia provider. There are bright lights, sounds from all the monitors, multiple people talking at the same time, metal instruments clanking, bone saws, hammering, and other sounds. It is quite the sensory experience.

When we started doing the clinical training in the operating room, I was having a rather difficult time seeing the "whole picture." I was also dealing with massive sensory overload. I assumed the others were experiencing everything just as I was, because I didn't realize my sensory problems were unlike others. I'd focus on one detail—for example, I'd need to start a second IV because there was going to be a lot of blood loss—so I would gather all the supplies needed to start the second IV and start working on securing it in the patient's hand. In the meantime, I'd forget to keep track of the many other critical things going on: the oxygen saturation, blood pressure, heart rate and rhythm, carbon dioxide level and waveform, depth of anesthesia, blood loss, progress of the surgery, rate the IV fluids were dripping at, degree of muscle relaxation (if necessary), inspiratory pressures of the ventilator, and keeping up with charting the anesthesia record, and more. You must keep high vigilance on all these areas throughout the case. When inducing anesthesia to put the patient off to "sleep," there are many things to keep track of, as well. The same is true when waking them up at the end of the case. So, I was facing the biggest challenge of achieving my goal of being a nurse anesthetist, which was being able to function in such a highly demanding, critical environment, a high level of multi-tasking, and the most extreme degree of executive functioning.

IF YOU'D LIKE TO KNOW MORE ABOUT AUTISM:

Executive function and multi-tasking are often problem areas for those on the autism spectrum. Basically, executive function and self-regulation skills are the mental processes that enable us to plan, focus attention, remember instructions, regulate our emotions, and juggle multiple tasks successfully.

For many on the autism spectrum, executive functioning is one of the most challenging tasks to achieve.

That's because EF issues are common to autism. According to research, those "with weak executive skills may:

- Have trouble starting and/or completing tasks
- Have difficulty prioritizing tasks
- Forget what they've just heard or read
- Have trouble following directions or creating a sequence of steps
- Panic when rules or routines change
- Have trouble switching focus from one task to another
- Get overly emotional and fixate on things
- Have trouble organizing their thoughts
- Have trouble keeping track of their belongings
- Not be able to manage their time

Since executive function develops over time, a[n individual] may struggle in different ways at different ages." [XXIV]

Some sources say that up to 80 percent of those on the autism spectrum suffer from executive function disorder. Remember, intelligence has no correlation with executive functioning; the individual may simply need to learn in a different way, so it may take a little longer.

I simply knew I felt overwhelmed. Because of the small class, it was one-on-one with each student with the instructor in the operating room. There was also an anesthesiologist present at induction and the waking up period at the end of each case. The instructors didn't know what to make of me, nor did I know what to make of them—except for one. She was a bit different herself. She kept to herself and didn't hang out with the other instructors. If it weren't for her intervention, I never would have made it through this grueling program. Her name was Carol.

Carol obviously recognized that I needed special guidance on working in the operating room. When she was with me, she'd sit on the floor and watch my every move. Instead of chastising me for things I overlooked or did wrong, she'd ask me a question to make me think of what it was I did or didn't do. She approached teaching in a very different way from the others.

One day, she took it even further. It was a Friday afternoon, around three-thirty, and all my classmates were already gone for the day. Carol said she'd like to talk to me in her office; I didn't know what to expect. Once sitting with her, she told me that she recognized I needed to learn things in a different way. She somehow saw that I needed to have everything broken down into small pieces, like a puzzle. She also stated that she knew I was unnecessarily "picked on" by the others. She said I'd need to try and ignore it and simply focus on what I needed to do for myself. Once she started helping me break things down into small pieces, it dawned on me to use visualization to put it all together, just as I had done for everything else I ever tackled.

This was the turning point of my training. Why I didn't think of using my visualization skills up until that point is beyond me. Perhaps I was just so stressed with everything, I couldn't see the trees for the forest. I simply didn't know what I didn't know, if that makes sense.

My assignment for the next day was a room full of pediatric cases. I had not yet done any pediatric anesthesia. All the drug dosages are obviously smaller, with different equipment and different techniques. When I first saw my assignment, I nearly fainted. My anxiety gripped me with all its might. I had a limited time to get this right.

CHAPTER 5

First, I made a list of everything I needed to do to get fully prepared for the next day. I tried not to focus on the fact that there was one instructor who was, I thought, obvious about his judgment of me as an idiot. I knew he would be looking for any and every misstep I'd take.

Second, I reviewed the chapter on pediatric anesthesia in the *Clinical Anesthesia Procedures of the Massachusetts General Hospital* handbook.

Third, I began visualizing. I visualized everything I'd be needing for each case, and I mean everything: each piece of equipment, drugs, the sequence of steps—every last detail. I reviewed these details over and over in my mind, as if I were actually doing the cases right then. I went to sleep feeling confident and ready to go.

The morning came quickly. I was in the operating room far earlier than necessary. That gave me extra time to visualize everything in "movie" version one last time before the start of the day. Finally, the big moment arrived. I effectively watched the movie in my mind, performing everything exactly as I had envisioned it. Each case went very smoothly, as if I'd done pediatrics my whole life. The instructor didn't say much of anything, and I wondered what he was thinking. After the last case ended, I headed back to the operating room to get my belongings. The instructor walked in, rested his elbows on the operating table, and looked at me. After what seemed an eternity he finally blurted out, "Well, I must say, I'm still in a state of shock. I knew this was going to be your first day doing pediatrics. I was expecting a total disaster. How is it that you suddenly have your act together today, especially for such a difficult thing? I felt like I was watching a totally different person."

I replied. "I visualized everything in my mind over and over last night. It prepared me for today."

Looking at me with his brows furrowed, he said, "Well, whatever you did, I can't believe what you did today. This is how to do it."

From that day forward, I visualized everything for all the cases the night before. My performance dramatically improved, and I continued working diligently toward earning my degree. Finally, the two (very long) years came to an end and graduation arrived. I felt very proud to have accomplished the rigorous program, and I learned a lot more than how to do anesthesia.

I actually activated my executive functioning skills through visualization. I couldn't have done it otherwise. I am still grateful all these years later to Carol, who believed in me and took the time to give me the help I so desperately needed. I realized that my ability to create a "movie" of what I needed to do, which incorporated all the details I needed to access and eliminated the "multi-functional imperative" the job called for. I simply had to pull up the images in the movie and check everything off, which was a life-saver for my career.

After graduating and taking my Board exam (which I passed the first time!), I began my career as a certified registered nurse anesthetist. My first job was at an inner-city hospital in Newark, New Jersey in 1988. It wasn't far from home, and at that time few hospitals in New Jersey were utilizing CRNAs. That was an experience in itself. When I worked on the in-hospital night call, was I got endless calls to go intubate patients in the intensive care units, the trauma unit, and emergency room anywhere from four to eight times a night. These patients weren't asleep like they are when in the operating room—they were awake, screaming, crying, and moving.

The nurses or doctors present would give them just a touch of sedation that would only last but a few moments; it did not knock them out, but it would simmer them down. All the intubating supplies would be ready to go when I'd arrive at the patient's bedside. I would have literally seconds to intubate the patient. It often meant life or death.

Back then, there wasn't fancy equipment like GlideScopes, which are available today. It was simply my skill, a laryngoscope, and an endotracheal tube. Talk about a lot of pressure. I didn't allow myself to get flustered; instead, I'd eyeball the patient's neck anatomy and imagine what their airway was going to look like once I was down their throat with the laryngoscope. That enabled me to be able to successfully pass that tube into their trachea on the first attempt.

I worked at that hospital for a year and a half. By the time I left, I felt as if I could intubate anyone, no matter how difficult their larynx anatomy was. I had developed numerous techniques to accommodate many airways, but it all boiled down to visualization.

In all situations, visualization was always my tool to get things done. I was drawn to specialties like neurosurgery because it had many details that necessitated visualization. I felt like my eyes had X-ray vision, seeing into the wrist or neck as to where to place the needle for anesthesia.

I do the same thing when I do spinals for orthopedic joint replacement surgery. As I'm prepping the patient's back with sterile sponge sticks, I'm already imagining their vertebrae to determine the angle in which to place the long spinal needle. In my mind's eye, I am seeing those vertebrae as if I'm an X-ray machine. I can insert the spinal needle and advance it until I feel the associated "pop," and then I remove the stylet to then inject the local anesthetic.

Visualization has enabled me to have my now-thirty-plus-year career as a CRNA. I truly believe that others can utilize this technique for whichever career path they choose. As you develop the visualization technique, you can use it for so many things you couldn't even imagine when you first began.

While I was interviewing Temple Grandin for my book *Temple Grandin: The Stories I Tell My Friends*, she told me about a program in Australia called Sun Pork, which strives to hire individuals on the autism spectrum to work on pig farms. Their program is unique. Instead of having the new hires start working on the farm with the pigs, they hold training workshops at a hotel in a big conference hall. Tables are set up with different learning areas. To learn to administer vaccinations to the pigs, they are given syringes with needles, vials with water to simulate vaccines, and oranges with cute little faces to represent pigs. Because the skin of an orange is very similar to that of a pig, the feel of giving the injection will simulate giving a real pig the injection.

The new employees learn how to draw up the "vaccine" in the syringes and inject it into the oranges. They must do it over and over until they feel comfortable doing it. Another thing they learn is how to put a tag on a pig's ear. That is simulated by using the hole-punching device on a piece of heavy cardboard and placing the tag on it. They must also wear the clothing they'd be wearing out on the actual farm, such as coveralls, muck boots, hats, and gloves to get acclimated to the feeling of the uniform.

Videos are shown of what it's like on the actual pig farm. This is intense training, and they do it repeatedly. This process allows them to visualize what they will be doing at their job before they even step foot on the pig farm.

Temple said it's a highly successful program. The new hires do extremely well in their new jobs because they have had the sensory experience and visualization to prepare them to deal with wiggling, squealing little piglets.

CHAPTER 5

DRIVING

Learning to drive is something that many on the autism spectrum have extreme difficulty with, are fearful of, and/or choose to delay learning or never learn at all. There are multiple factors involved with this, safety being the most critical one.

Not only do you have to master handling the vehicle, but then you must go out on the road with other vehicles all around you. Even if you learn to drive the car or truck, on the road you never know what other drivers are going to do. There is also the issue of spatial orientation and depth perception, both of which give trouble to most with ASD. It is an overwhelming experience and should never be forced upon any individual on the spectrum. Driving is something you must personally decide you are ready to do. Otherwise, it could be disastrous.

For example, I know of a family that literally forced their seventeen-year-old daughter with Asperger's to get her driver's learning permit. The girl just wasn't ready emotionally. Intellectually, she was extremely bright, but intelligence doesn't have anything to do with driving. So, the girl learned at her high school along with her classmates. When they took her out on the main road, she panicked, confused the gas pedal for the break, and plowed into another vehicle. Fortunately, no one was seriously injured, at least not physically. The girl was so shaken by the event that she refused to ever drive again. The parents initially thought she was simply being obstinate, but the reality was that the girl recognized she wasn't ready to attempt driving.

Here's my advice to all parents: never try to force your ASD child to learn to drive. I have a dynamic presentation about how to go about teaching the individual on the spectrum how to drive when they are ready.

BECOMING AN AUTISM SUCCESS STORY

When I was in high school, they taught the students how to drive, enabling us to get our learner's permit and then to go for the written and road tests to get a driver's license. Looking back, I'm surprised I ever even attempted to do it. The school thought the best way to put the fear of God in everyone was to show a movie that showed the dangers of driving. The opening scene was a woman and her daughter in their home. They were hosting an estate sale, with dozens of people milling about, buying every last piece of furniture they had. I was confused as to what it was all about. Then, a customer asked the woman why they were selling everything, so she told her story of the sunny afternoon she, her husband, daughter, and son were on their way home from church. They were all smiling and chattering about the sermon. Suddenly, a drunk driver came careening around a blind corner and crashed head on into their car. There was screaming, the horrific sound of metal colliding, then silence. As the cloud of black smoke began to settle, you then see two dead bodies, her husband and son. No longer able to afford their home, she was forced to sell the home and the contents. The school succeeded in scaring me. Maybe other students didn't see in pictures and have that film etched in their mind forever. On the other hand, maybe that's why I'm a totally conservative driver who follows all the rules of the road.

We were taught to drive over the next eight weeks, first in the classroom, then in simulator cars with movie screens in front of them, and finally out on the road. I was actually having fun in the simulator cars, all located in a large, dimly lit room. It all seemed like a piece of cake...until the day I started the ignition on the real car.

I was going to have my first session with the instructor out on the road. Being in a simulator was quite different from being in a real car. I was totally overwhelmed with all the other vehicles

CHAPTER 5

whizzing all around me. I proceeded to go along with it, despite being gripped with fear. I hated every second behind the wheel.

I completed all the school's training then went for my driver's license written and road tests. I passed both. I drove minimally for the next few months, only to the store and back. One day, I got my first experience with road rage. Someone in a fast car flew right up to the back of my car. I knew I wasn't going fast enough for them. They rode my tail a few minutes, then shot around me and cut right in front of me. I had to slam on my brakes or I would have hit him. That shook me to the core. When I pulled into the driveway and shut off the ignition, I took the keys and handed them to my mom. I stated I was done with driving, and that was that for the next twenty-three years.

I walked to the first college I attended, as it was in my town and not too far away (Bloomfield College in New Jersey). When I was going to start at Montclair State College (now Montclair State University), my mom learned to drive. From then on, she drove me everywhere I needed to go. Prior to her driving, my dad took me everywhere. Many years later, once I discovered I'm on the autism spectrum, we realized mom was, too. That was why she had never learned to drive in her younger days.

At college, no one knew my mom drove me there. Once I started working as a CRNA, people began to see that I was being dropped off and picked up by my mom. That provided a lot of fuel for bullying and harassment in the workplace, but I still wasn't motivated to want to start driving again.

One day, everything changed. My mom hurt her knee and had to be on total bedrest for three weeks. I was forty at the time. She thought of it first: how was I going to get to and from work? My dad was getting early stages of Alzheimer's, so I had just recently taken away his driver's license and vehicle keys. It was very hard to do that, but if I wanted to keep him and everyone on the road safe, I had to.

The realization hit me. I had no choice. The time had come that I had to start driving. I recall retreating to a comfortable chair, closing my eyes so I could begin visualizing everything from walking out to the truck, starting it up, and getting out on the road. I imagined driving to and from work. I visualized everything: the feel of the steering wheel, my right foot on the gas pedal, the switch to the brake. All the landmarks along the way. Glancing down at the gauges to check my speed, amount of gas in the tank, the water and oil gauges, watching for traffic lights, every last detail. I spent quite a long time visualizing all of this, several hours at least, over and over and over and over. I kept doing it until I felt comfortable and secure, as if I'd been doing it the past twenty-three years. Finally, I felt ready.

I didn't want to wait until the next morning to drive to work. I decided to go to the grocery store. I went and, as I expected, I felt as if I had been driving all those years. Now I realize that by visualizing it so many times, it either re-activated what I had stored away or I created a new conduit in my brain to be able to drive without fear.

I believe that by using visualization techniques, many people on the autism spectrum can successfully learn to drive without having the great anxiety typically associated with driving.

ON BECOMING AN AUTISM ACTIVIST

I will always remember that fateful night at work when I discovered I'm on the autism spectrum. This was the greatest gift I ever received, learning why I am the way I am. To have gone fifty years not knowing *why* had caused a lot of stress, because I was always searching for answers. I had never encountered anyone else like myself at that point except, of course, my mom. I was just like her. It would take a few more years to recognize she, too, had Asperger's. For my mom, learning I had Asperger's took the weight of the world off her shoulders. She had shed many tears thinking she had done something wrong in raising me because I was so different. She saw all my struggles and the abuse I endured from the outside world, even as an adult. She carried tremendous guilt all those years. Now, finally, she was free. I can remember the night I came home from work with all those books and the big news of the Asperger's. We cried tears of happiness for hours.

Over the next three weeks I read all the books I had bought and made an appointment with the same neuropsychologist my co-worker had taken her son to. I then received my formal diagnosis after all the testing, which took several sessions.

So, there it was, a piece of paper in my hand stating I had Asperger's. In 2013 the new *Diagnostic and Statistical Manual of Mental Disorders, 5th Edition* (DSM-5) lumped Asperger's into the umbrella of autism spectrum disorders (ASD), so I then began referring to myself as having autism.

I didn't waste any time moving on my new perspective. I immediately began visualizing what I needed to do: help others on the autism spectrum. I wanted to do this on a global scale. Just like everything else I'd done, I wanted to do it *big*. This wasn't going to be any different! I embarked on a journey that's growing bigger and better every day.

The first thing I did was write a memoir, *Asperger's Syndrome: When Life Hands You Lemons, Make Lemonade*. That was cathartic to me. This was the book Temple Grandin saw, and it inspired her to contact me about including me in her book *Different…Not Less*. I also started an autism support group in my community which I ran for many years.

I had the great honor of being a guest speaker at the United Nations Headquarters in New York City for World Autism Awareness Day in 2017. Being invited to speak there was one of the most exciting events of my life, it was incredible. It was a very cold March morning in New York City, and there was a cold mist in the air. Walking up to that spectacular building, seeing the flags from all over the world, and entering the great amphitheater room to see my name all lit up still makes my hair stand on end. It would have been easy to become overwhelmed by it all, yet I had visualized remaining calm, and that's exactly what I did. When it was my time to speak, I simply spoke from my heart, like I always do. I didn't focus on the thousands of people in the room, nor the cameras live-streaming the event around the world. As I was there, I did think to myself of the far road I've traveled, from the poor kid with the coal miner grandpa, to speaking on a stage at the United Nations. That truly was a moment that stood still, enabling me to see that anything is possible in life if you are willing to work for it. I recently did a keynote at the Federal Communications Commission in Washington, DC for National Employees with Disabilities Month. I speak all over the country at autism conferences as well, many along with Dr. Temple Grandin. I always visualize my presentations over and over, so when I actually do them, I feel like I've done it hundreds of times!

CHAPTER 5

CHANGING HEALTH CARE FOR ALL ON THE AUTISM SPECTRUM

My entire life, long before I got my diagnosis, I recognized that I had very unpleasant experiences concerning anything to do with doctors, dentists, or any type of health care issues. Just the thought of going in for a check-up would send me into a tailspin. I knew I'd have to sit in a cramped, noisy, brightly lit waiting area with dozens of people. It would be too hot for me, and more than one person would reek of perfume, cologne, or cigarette smoke. There would likely be a TV blasting, many people talking, and health care providers periodically entering the waiting area to yell out the next patient's name. That in itself always sent me into a meltdown. If you go to some fast food restaurants, after you place your order, they give you a buzzer that will vibrate and light up when your food is ready. At a doctor's office, first they make you sign all kinds of forms regarding HIPAA and Privacy violations. Then a nurse comes out to the crowded waiting area and yells out your name so that everyone hears it. Where's the privacy? Instead, each patient should be given a buzzer that lights up when it's your turn to get called back to the exam room! After what would seem an eternity, it would be my turn to get called, and I'd follow the nurse down the long corridor and into an exam room. There they would proceed to take my blood pressure, heart rate, temperature, and oxygen saturation. The worker typically appeared frazzled, and did everything in a hurried fashion, generally while not uttering a peep. Then they would ask me a few questions as to the nature of my visit, enter my responses into my chart, and then turn to leave the room while stating that the doctor would be in shortly. I'd sit there for another eternity, all the while my anxiety building. The lights would be so bright I'd have to keep my eyes squinted or shut in order to tolerate sitting there.

BECOMING AN AUTISM SUCCESS STORY

Health care providers never seemed to understand me or take me seriously. At times, I felt that they didn't even treat me with respect. By not understanding autism, health care providers don't understand their patient: how to communicate with us, the numerous special needs we may have, or specific health care requirements (like not reacting to medications like others do). Before I was diagnosed with a autism, I thought I was the only person to ever experience all these negative, overwhelming things. Yet, after my discovery, and meeting endless people on the autism spectrum, I began hearing these same exact experiences from all of them. I realized the cause of all this. It was very simple: health care providers lack knowledge about autism. Once I began delving into this arena, I even found research studies which showed that health care providers admitted to lacking adequate knowledge to provide quality care to this population.

I had an "a-ha!" moment when I realized that I have the capability to build a bridge between these two worlds, health care providers and individuals on the autism spectrum. By combining my thirty years of experience as a medical professional with my life's experience with autism, I wrote the book *The Complete Guide to Autism and Healthcare*. We are striving to continue getting this book into medical schools, nursing programs, and all health care facilities around the world. I also continue to visualize the positive impact this book will have for the future of those on the autism spectrum. Everyone wants to be treated with dignity and respect, and everyone wants to receive the best care possible. Unless all health care providers have this knowledge and understanding, they are not able to provide the same level of care that all others receive. I am very excited that my book has already begun to make its way into medical schools and other health care facilities as required reading. To further facilitate educating health care providers, I speak at health care facilities and conferences around the country.

Many individuals on the autism spectrum have co-existing conditions, me included. Most of us have anxiety, which can easily exacerbate any and all of a person's other conditions. Health care providers need to learn that yes, autism is in our mind, but it affects the rest of our body.

I also am hopeful that the concept of visualization and neuro-plasticity is going to be the new wave for the autism world. As an autism activist, my goal is to enable others to reach their highest potential by rewiring their brains. My goal is for everyone to have happy, productive, and fulfilling lives.

VISUALIZING MY WAY TO A FLIGHT IN A F-15 FIGHTER JET

I was living in Wisconsin in my early thirties when, on a snowy Friday, I decided to stop in a video rental store on my way home from work. It was not something I typically did. I didn't have any-thing in mind to see, so I simply wandered around to see if any-thing struck my fancy. I had looked up and down all the aisles, and nothing appealed to me. Heading down the last one, I spotted *Top Gun*. It had been released in 1986, but I'm not a movie-goer, so I never saw it. Maybe it was Tom Cruise's mega-watt smile, the flight suit decorated with colorful patches, or the cockpit of the jet that caught my eye. Whatever it was, that was the movie I wanted to watch! Once home, I built a nice, crackling fire in the fireplace, made some popcorn, and settled on the couch, ready to be enter-tained. Little did I know that, by the time the film was over, my life was about to take a very different turn. As the movie went on,

BECOMING AN AUTISM SUCCESS STORY

I realized it wasn't Tom Cruise or his smile, nor the flight suits. It was the fighter jets themselves that lured me into reaching for that movie in the store. The more scenes I saw of those incredible, multi-million-dollar jets performing maneuvers that seemed impossible, the more intrigued I became. My mom was watching the movie with me and she was getting a little bit concerned with my extreme interest in the high-performance aircraft. She already sensed a flame had been ignited deep inside of me. She knew that when I became interested in something, it turned into an obsession that I focused my whole being on. By the end of the movie, I announced to her that I wanted to fly in a fighter jet! I can still see the look on her face. It wasn't pretty.

Realizing it was basically impossible for a civilian to get a flight in a military fighter jet, I had to think for weeks about how I could accomplish this feat. I subscribed to every magazine on military aviation that I could find. I feverishly read each one, cover to cover, retaining every last detail. It was all I could think about.

I began visualizing myself in the back seat of a fighter jet, taking off down the runway with a full after-burner take off. This was more difficult to visualize, because I didn't have the sensory input to refer to; this visualization was totally dependent on the movie I'd seen, so I didn't have aspects like smells or vestibular experiences to include. I learned you can still visualize without those things, but it's much more difficult.

One day, I discovered there was the 115th Fighter Wing that housed the Wisconsin Air National Guard located at Dane County Regional Airport in Madison, Wisconsin—very close to where I lived. They had a squadron of F-16's. I was able to find out what time they took off on Saturday mornings, and that was my first encounter with seeing actual fighter jets in action.

CHAPTER 5

The military jets were located on the opposite side of the airport, away from the commercial aircrafts. We found the road which led down to the squadron area. It was a freezing January morning but I was already out of the truck, running up to the tall chain link fence. I stuck my fingers through the openings and clung on to see the thrilling scene before me. There were six F-16 fighter jets neatly lined up on the flight line. The pilots were walking out of the building looking sharp in their flight suits. The ground crew were busy at the jets, getting everything ready for the pilots. I saw the pilots climb up the ladders to their respective jets and enter the cockpits.

Soon they were running up their engines and taxiing out to the runway. I was near hysteria with excitement; they were so close that I could see the pilots faces! One by one, they rolled down the runway, accelerating rapidly and lifting off. As they each started barreling down the runway, the sound from the engines was overwhelming and the ground shook like an earthquake was rumbling under my feet. I was jumping up and down squealing in delight!

I started crying tears of joy, which were literally freezing as they began running down my cheeks. It was a spectacular sensory experience. All of my senses were maxed out by the smell of the jet fuel, the roar of the engines, the ground-splitting sensations. Now I had the "real thing" to take home and use to expand upon my visualization. Everything clicked as real, which was far more thrilling than seeing it in a movie.

After that first encounter alongside the fence, I was fueled by my thrill. I'd visualize getting geared up into a flight suit, the G-suit, putting a helmet into a flight bag, neatly folding the flight gloves, then tucking them into my G-suit. I visualized walking out into the cold, crisp air and to the F-16 awaiting my arrival. I envisioned slowly climbing up the ladder and climbing into the back seat. I "saw" the canopy come down and lock into place. I visualized taxiing out to the runway, and felt the acceleration and the shot of adrenaline as we took off into the skies. I'd go through this "movie" in my mind over and over for years. Again, it was from two perspectives, that of me watching myself, and then from my own perspective. Each time, all my senses came alive, savoring each and every tiny detail, right down to the smell of the jet fuel.

I wasn't interested in becoming a fighter pilot, only to fly in one of those high-performance aircrafts.

Where there's a will, there's a way. I concluded that one way to get onto the bases where the fighter jets were located would be to write articles for the numerous military aviation magazines I admired and read each month. At first, I had no clue what I was doing. I would read each article and analyze how they were structured and the kinds of information they contained. I believed I could start writing similar articles, so I began contacting some of the magazines and offering to send them articles. They were all very receptive.

I was now three years into my venture, when a magazine arrived with travel suggestions in it. It had a two-page spread of Pensacola, Florida. One whole page was a photo of the U.S. Navy Blue Angels in formation. The other page showed the beautiful white sands of Pensacola Beach and the emerald green and turquoise water of the Gulf of Mexico. It wasn't the beach scene that got me. It was the Blue Angels. When I learned that their home base was the Naval Air Station Pensacola, that was it! I also saw that Eglin Air Force Base, home of the 33rd Fighter Wing, was not very far away from there. The existence of those bases were huge magnets pulling me down there, so I made a decision.

I announced to mom and dad that we were moving to Florida! Within a week, I had job interviews lined up and mom and I were flying down from Wisconsin to Pensacola. I can still recall our flights to and from Pensacola on an airline called Mid-West Express. Their gimmick was serving freshly baked chocolate chip cookies that they actually baked on the plane, right after the meal was served. In fact, their meals were delicious, served on real china dishes with real silverware and lovely glasses to drink from. When they baked the cookies, that aroma went wafting throughout the entire aircraft, making everyone salivate. I got hired at a job to work as a nurse anesthetist full time, found a place to keep my horses, and found a home all in one week.

Once back up in Wisconsin, I went into overdrive orchestrating the move. One month later, I sold the home in which my parents and I lived, packed up my parents and all my animals, and moved 1,000 miles south to the northwest corner of the Florida panhandle. What a whirlwind! Typically, us folk on the autism spectrum don't tolerate any sort of change very well—except, that is, when you desperately want something. Then you can override everything and just go for it!

I'd never written an article for a magazine or even owned a good quality camera, both of which I needed gain access to the military bases, conduct interviews with the pilots and ground crews, and photograph the jets. I was used to using disposable cameras from the neighborhood pharmacy. To capture military jets traveling at nearly 500 mph, I had to get a camera and lenses that could photograph speed. I bought a Nikon F-5, because that seemed to be what the military aviation photojournalists who regularly wrote for the magazines I was reading were using. This camera was pretty complicated, but that didn't stop me. I had in my head the kind of photos I needed to have to go with the articles I would be writing. Basically, I knew nothing of F-stops or any fancy photography talk. It was simply point and shoot.

BECOMING AN AUTISM SUCCESS STORY

I could gain entry at NAS Pensacola to see the Blue Angels practice with the thousands of people who flocked there each Tuesday and Wednesday morning to watch and capture photos. I would go there praying to get even just one good photo. I'd routinely take dozens, go to the one-hour photo developing counter at the drugstore, and nervously wait in my truck to see my results. Back in 1998, there were no such things as digital cameras, so I with stuck with 35mm film roll that had to be developed.

At first, the photos only showed a pretty blue sky—not even a hint of a jet—but even that didn't discourage me. I'd watch other photographers so I could visualize how to hold the camera better and how to "lock on" to the jets when I looked through the lens. I saw a lot of blue sky in my photos until, one day, it all changed.

The guy at the film counter who developed all those blue-sky photos had a huge grin on his face that day. As I walked back into the store from my truck, he blurted out, "I think you're going to be pretty surprised at your photos today!" Photo after photo, the Blue Angels jets were in flight, captured both in formation and when the solo pilots did their thing. I was beside myself. Finally, my visualization with the camera enabled me to be able to capture these images. From then on, I never had a problem photographing the jets, whether going at high rates of speed, looping, flying in formations, landing, or suiting up.

I spent the next four years diligently writing articles and providing photos for the magazines to become an internationally published military aviation photojournalist. I still maintained working full time at my job as an anesthetist, although I used all my vacation time, weekends, and evenings to pursue this special interest.

I also made my way into spending time with the squadron of the world's most elite flight demonstration team, the U.S. Navy

CHAPTER 5

Blue Angels. Meeting all the Blue Angel pilots and the entire squadron was very thrilling. These six pilots fly eighteen inches apart at speeds over 500 mph. They have nerves of steel. I can still remember their high-octane energy which matched their high-performance jets, the F-18 Hornets. They knew the extreme teamwork and trust necessary to fly in that environment. I learned a lot from my time spent there, not only about the jets but life skills, as well. They, too, used visualization to prepare for each flight demonstration.

On my first visit to Eglin AFB as a writer, they took me out to the flight line in a "bread truck," which indeed looks like an old-fashioned bread delivery truck. Inside there are benches all around the perimeter, which the fighter pilots sit on for the ride out to the jets.

So, there I sat, amidst a squadron of real-life fighter pilots donned in their flight suits, G-suits, tons of safety gear, with their helmets tucked under their arm. *Wow!* I soaked it all in. They were exchanging comments about the sortie (training mission) they were about to fly out over the Gulf of Mexico. It was truly a spectacular event for me.

As the truck made its final turn, the flight line became visible. There they were: dozens of F-15's neatly lined up in numerous rows. The truck pulled up right in front of the line, stopped to allow several pilots to get out, then went on down the line to let off the remaining pilots.

These were the best-of-the-best fighter pilots in the world and there I was, right along with them. This particular day I was going to be doing a photo shoot for an article I was writing about the fighter wing. It was a cold November day, and the wind was pretty snappy and cold, but the excitement of seeing all the fighter pilots climbing up into their jets was keeping me quite warm.

Each jet had multiple ground crews tending to all the pre-flight checks and getting the pilots hooked up inside the cockpit. They had to ensure the pilot was properly hooked up to the ejection seat, along with the oxygen hose and his G-suit. There was so much to see all at once and I was snapping away, capturing the essence of everything happening right in front of me.

They allowed me to get right up to the jets to feel them and experience the thrill as each jet was started, running intense vibrations through the ground. I was given ear covers to wear, but I could still hear the roar of twenty fighter jets going. I was beside myself. My dream was starting to come true. It certainly wouldn't be hard to imagine the sensory stimuli the jets created any longer.

Several years later, after visiting Eglin Air Force Base numerous times, I was shooting photos and interviewing the pilots for my articles when one of the two squadrons (the 33rd Fighter Wing's Fighting Crows) informed me that I had been named their honorary squadron commander! They had adopted me as their squadron mascot years before, so I was happy to have been selected for their squadron's elevated position.

Then, the big news came: they told me that I was going to get to fly in one of their F-15 Strike Eagles as their honorary squadron commander! When I heard the news, I felt an incredible adrenalin rush from head to toe. I was actually going to be able to fly in one of the F-15 Fighter jets! I had never given up on my dream of flying, and now it was going to become a reality.

That day, I stood there photographing each jet as it raced down the runway and disappeared into the cloudy sky. As I was soon to learn, seeing it happen can't even begin to compare with the thrilling feeling you experience when you are in the aircraft.

In the seven years leading up to my flight, I had the luxury of

CHAPTER 5

spending time in the secret world of fighter jet pilots. I was invited to join them in their squadron bar, the Crow's Nest. It truly was just like a scene in a movie, with fighter pilots packed inside, the walls plastered with photos of fighter jets and various mementos, and a huge air hockey game table in the middle of the room. There was music playing and conversation filled the room. Many of the pilots had two red plastic cups, one in each hand. I soon came to learn that one was filled with draft beer and the other was to spit the juice from the chewing tobacco wadded in the sides of their mouths. (The thought did cross my mind, what would happen if they accidentally took a sip from the cup filled with the chew spit? Ew!) The aroma in the Crow's Nest was a mixture of beer, sweat, whiskey, and cologne. I wandered around and mingled amongst them, listening to one aviation experience after another. Just like Maverick and Ice Man in *Top Gun*, all these fighter pilots would flail their hands and arms around, simulating their jets and maneuvers. I couldn't get enough of it all.

A week before my flight, I was required to spend two days going through survival training.

This included going on the ejection seat simulator, learning how to come down in a parachute, suiting up in full flight regalia and all the safety equipment, climbing up the tall ladder into the cockpit of an F-15, and spending an hour in a real F-15 flight simulator run by instructors from the Boeing corporation. I also had to learn how to breathe with the G-pressure suit, how to evacuate in the event of a fire on the ground, and how to respond if there was a major malfunction in the air. I had to learn the lingo: the pilot's command "Egress! Egress! Egress!" or "Bail out, bail out, bail out!" There was a low probability of the need for any such events, but it was necessary to know. That in itself was a thrilling experience!

BECOMING AN AUTISM SUCCESS STORY

The ejection seat simulator was a real ejection seat attached to a fifty-foot track up to the ceiling on a slight incline. With my full flight gear on, they harnessed me into the seat. Once ready, I was to pull an ominous-looking, yellow and black handle with the words "pull to eject" on it. There was one in front of the seat between my legs and another along the side of the ejection seat. It didn't matter which one you pulled, either one was going to ignite the rockets attached to the sides of the seat which would blast you out of the cockpit like a rocket bound for outer space. They explained to rest my head back on the seat; otherwise, I could get a fractured vertebra in my neck. Once it was all ready, I pulled the handle and off I blasted to the top of the track. It took my breath away! It was loud and exhilarating—talk about an adrenalin rush. I have to admit, I've been known to be an adrenalin junkie. I wanted to do it again, and they let me! I was like a little kid on Christmas morning, grinning ear to ear. What a blast…literally!

Next came the parachute jump. I had to get on an elevator that took me up several stories to a platform; It wasn't for the faint of heart. Once up there, my flight harness cables were hooked up to simulate a parachute. There were several components to this training. On the ground they taught me how to untwist my parachute lines if I went into a spin. They also taught me how to reach into the pocket of my flight suit to get the pocket knife if I needed to cut my lines free, assuming I landed in a tree or on power lines. Once ready, I stepped off the platform for my descent. It was like free falling for a few moments; then, when the parachute opened, it swooped me upwards in a thrilling sensation. I floated down toward the Earth. They twisted my chute to give me the opportunity to untwist my lines. I reached up, grabbing each set of lines, and twisted with all my might to get myself straightened out.

CHAPTER 5

Next, it was on to the building where the fighter pilots did their special training in the Boeing F-15 flight simulators. The simulators were in an actual cockpit of F-15's. I excitedly climbed in, hooked up, and was ready to take the controls. At home, over those seven years, I had spent hundreds of hours on my flight simulator software. I even had a joystick and rudders. I could "fly" quite well. The flight instructor suggested I was ready to be hired by the United States Air Force Thunderbirds!

Finally, the big day arrived. I was up before the sun rose, hyperventilating at the thought that the flight I had been visualizing for seven years was finally here! I ate dry toast and some coffee. I was thinking whatever I ate would probably be coming back up at some point during the flight.

I arrived early at the fighter wing. My mom and I were staying at a hotel right outside the gate of Eglin Air Force Base. She came with me to watch me get into the F-15 and take off. She was pale from anxiety. I knew she was hoping I'd chicken out and not do it. Fat chance of that happening. I parked at the back door of the squadron building and off I went to get suited and rigged up by a team of personnel. I was savoring every moment. I had arrived with the flight suit already on, so they rigged me up with the parachute harness, G-suit, and a pocket knife, placing it inside a pocket on my thigh. They had me put on my helmet to ensure the oxygen mask fit perfectly. I was ready to go. Now it was time for the pre-flight briefing with the colonel who was going to fly the jet.

The briefing took place in a conference room down the hall from the Crow's Nest and lasted over an hour. The base had commissioned two photographers to capture my entire experience on both film and video. They were both in that room capturing my facial expressions as the briefing went on. Although I was never much for facial expressions, I was making plenty during that session. It was basically a safety briefing of all the many things that could go wrong during the flight, and what would happen if they did. I will admit that, as he went deeper and deeper into the graphic details of peril, I did have some fleeting moments of second thoughts. The videographer had zoomed in on my face and it was obvious what I was thinking, but I quickly talked myself out of my reservations. The pilot smiled and told me to relax so I could enjoy my flight of a lifetime.

I had full confidence in my pilot. He had thousands of flight hours in the F-15, had flown combat missions, and would be in full command of that jet. I had to sign a standard liability release and undergo a strict physical exam by the flight surgeon on the base to determine I was fit enough to endure the flight. I was thankful to pass it.

We all walked out en masse to the bread truck waiting for us outside. I quickly ran over to my truck and reassured my mom that I'd be okay. She forced a smile and said she was going to sit there and pray the whole time. They actually brought her right out to the flight line, but I didn't learn that until later.

On the ride out to the jets, the colonel reviewed some things he talked about during the briefing. He was chewing gum a hundred miles an hour. I asked him what he had for breakfast. Two cups of black coffee, he replied. I should have guessed. The truck pulled up to our jet. There it was, looming right before my eyes, our F-15 Strike Eagle fighter jet. Of course, I'd seen the F-15's many times, but today I was going to be in one for an incredible flight. It had a symbol painted on it near the tail, which signified it had flown in Operation Desert Storm. Wow. A real war plane. I was teetering on being overwhelmed, ready to explode with excitement and with a sense of empowerment because I was minutes away from my ultimate achievement. I can remember every detail to this day.

The pilot had me walk with him as he performed the walk-around that each pilot does before each flight. The ground crew was scurrying about, tending to last-minute details. There was a huge fuel line hooked up to the jet, filling the fuel tanks. The smell of jet fuel was perfume to my nose. The McDonnell Douglas F-15 Strike Eagle is "an American twin-engine, all-weather tactical fighter aircraft designed by McDonnell Douglas (now Boeing) to gain and maintain air supremacy in all aspects of aerial combat."[XXV] It is a thirty-million-dollar fighter jet. My pilot determined that all systems were a go.

The pilot climbed up the narrow ladder and into the cockpit. The ground crew hooked up his safety gear, oxygen hose, and reviewed final checks. I walked over to the steep, narrow ladder and slowly made my way up. I didn't look down at the ground, I eagerly climbed over the side and into the cockpit. My senses were in over-drive. The ground crew was focused on getting me all hooked up. I put on my helmet and mask, and they hooked up the oxygen hose to my mask. My helmet was also equipped with a radio, so the pilot and I could be in full communication throughout the flight. I could hear everything he was saying to the ground crew. I was starting to hyperventilate. He heard that, looked in the tiny rearview mirror at me, and told me to relax. He then looked one more time at me, asked if I was ready, and when I said yes he gave a thumbs-up.

I saw him reach over to touch the switch that made the canopy of the jet start coming down. It made a very distinct hydraulic sound as it slowly lowered down to the jet frame, then slid forward, making a locking and hissing sound. I was looking out at the ground crew pulling the chocks away from the wheels. Once they were all clear of the aircraft, the pilot slowly started pulling forward to head out to the runway. I looked down at my flight suit, my hands clad in fighter pilot gloves, examining the entire cockpit, and smelling the jet fuel. My adrenalin was running full speed.

We taxied out to the runway, then sat there a few minutes. He explained he was waiting for clearance from the air tower. Suddenly, in my helmet I heard a voice declare, "Crow 5-1 ready for take-off!" With that, he released the brakes, causing the massive jet to lurch forward as he swung us out onto to actual runway. From the back seat, I could see him pushing the throttle as we then began hurling down the runway, covered in black streaks from all the thousands of times the fighter jets had taken off and landed on it before. I had never seen a runway of a fighter wing from that perspective, so that was thrilling, too. As we gained speed, over 200 mph, he started lighting the after burners. There were five in total. As each flame ignited, it produced a massive "punch" behind us, like getting kicked by an elephant from behind. I counted them, *one, two, three, four, five.* I could feel the extreme power of the aircraft as we went straight up to 15,000 feet. The G-force was much more intense than I could have ever imagined. As I sat in the back seat of that magnificent flying machine roaring down the runway, I smiled to myself thinking of the hundreds, probably thousands of times I had visualized that moment. Now, it was truly happening.

The higher we climbed, the harder it was to breathe. It felt like a truck was pouring concrete all over my body. The force was so intense that I couldn't even lift up my hand. I did perform the exercises I had learned earlier: a type of "hook" pressure breathing, where I had to squeeze my lower extremities. It helped keep most of the blood in my head. The G-suit inflated around my legs, which also helped. I was relieved that I didn't pass out. I didn't even get the

CHAPTER 5

tunnel vision that some people apparently get. At 15,000 feet, my pilot rolled the jet over backward, made a loop, then leveled it out. There were a few moments of the sensation of free falling.

I then got nauseated and felt the need to quickly unhook my face mask, reach for the plastic bag neatly tucked into the front of my G-suit for just such an occasion. Out came that toast and black coffee. The pilot was looking at me in his mirror. How embarrassing. I was told it happens to even the best pilots when they are not at the controls. I quickly tied up the bag as instructed and dropped it on the floor between my combat boots.

Once settled down, I looked out at the beautiful blue sky and the fluffy white clouds. Nothing can compare with looking out of the crystal-clear cockpit canopy, which enhances the surrealism of it all. Here I was, in the back seat of one of America's most sophisticated supersonic fighter jets, with one of the best fighter pilots in the whole world. I wanted that moment to last forever. It was a pinnacle moment of my life.

After ensuring I was okay, the pilot performed the next maneuver, going just under supersonic. He eased the nose of the plane up and accelerated to Mach .95. I didn't feel much except for more G-force. He instructed me to look at the tachometer, the speedometer, to see we were just a hair under Mach 1, the speed of sound. I looked down at the ground 15,000 feet below. It didn't really look much different than peering out the window on all my commercial flights, but it did have a *feeling* of speed. Yes, I did mutter that famous line from *Top Gun*, "I feel the need, the need for speed!"

It seemed like a fleeting moment before we were heading back to the base. I started feeling nauseated again, probably because we were coming in about fifty feet over Loxahatchee Bay. There were boaters looking up, and I could count their eyelashes because we were so close to them. I was happy when I felt the wheels touch down on that black-streaked runway. Arriving at the fighter wing jet tarmac, the jet came to a stop, and the canopy opened with that hydraulic sound again. After a few minutes I got up and began my descent down that narrow ladder. Once my feet were planted on the ground, I shook hands with my pilot and profusely thanked him.

The party wasn't quite over yet.

The next event was not something I expected. We all climbed back into the bread truck to return to the squadron building. Once there, I was escorted to the Crow's Nest. As it turned out, the tradition is that, after you get a flight in one of their fighter jets, you must partake in a shot of their special whiskey, Jeremiah Weed. Whiskey? It was ten-thirty in the morning, and I had never had whiskey. Well, what could I do? There was no choice.

They cheerfully poured me a shot glass full and handed it to me. I slugged it down in one fast gulp. Good grief, it tasted like paint thinner. They were cheering for me. Within a few moments, I started feeling a warm buzz from head to toe.

So, I had done it. I had flown in an F-15 fighter jet (and drank their whiskey, too)! It was a thrill of a lifetime.

Now, I'm simply happy to watch my video of that incredible day. It's like experiencing it all over again. Even without watching the video, I can feel it, just like I can when I visualized it in my mind. I wouldn't be very interested in flying in an F-15 again, but I admit I wouldn't turn down a flight from the U.S. Navy Blue Angels or the U.S. Air Force Thunderbirds.

For those who dream of getting a flight in a fighter jet, you can…if you have $25,000 cash to spare plus all expenses to fly to Russia, where they offer that thrill of a lifetime. My flight in an F-15 Strike Eagle fighter jet took seven years to achieve, but far exceeded my expectations. I truly believe I would never have achieved such a spectacular goal if I had not visualized my way there!

THE SNOWFLAKE RIDE

There are moments in one's life that are remembered forever. The "snowflake ride," as I call it, was one of those times for me. I want to share this experience with you. This was on my beloved horse, Lars. I was living in Wisconsin at the time, and it was the first day of April. It was a cold morning, right at thirty-two degrees. I took Lars out of his stall and put him on the cross ties to brush him, put on the saddle, and take him outside to ride. Just as I led him out, a herd of deer came running down the hill next to the barn. There were about ten of them, traveling swiftly, their white tails up. It was quite a sight of those majestic animals, very exhilarating. They created a thunderous sound as they ran through all the trees, causing Lars to start cavorting around me, snorting as he, too, watched the deer. It caused quite an adrenalin rush for both of us.

I was enjoying the frigid air and the vapor coming from my mouth and Lars' nostrils. The air smelled so fresh and clean; all of my senses were alive and taking in every luxurious detail around me. As I got on, I settled down into the saddle, listening to the special sound the leather made as my riding boots rested against it. I let Lars walk around the arena for a while to relax after our deer encounter. Once we were both ready, I gathered up the reins and prepared to begin working. Collected canter was our favorite thing to do, so instead of warming up at the trot, I decided to ask him for a canter. He stepped into his huge, rolling canter, and I sat back in the saddle to tell him to slow down. He instantly sat deeper on his haunches, slowed down, and went into his spectacular collected canter. Lars was a half thoroughbred, half Clydesdale and stood at eighteen hands. For those not familiar with what this means, if you are standing next to him, his back was at about six feet tall. I needed a mounting block to get on him. He weighed in at 2,500 pounds and his markings were those of a Budweiser Clydesdale. He was a real show-stopper, and he loved people. Our bond was as close as a human can get with an animal, and we were like one being when riding. That made this experience all the grander.

It wasn't unusual to get snow in April up in Wisconsin. As we were cantering along, huge snowflakes began to gently come down all around us. They were the biggest snowflakes I'd ever seen, about the size of silver dollars. I put my arm out to catch some snowflakes on my black jacket. I inspected them, amazed at the intricate beauty of each flake crystal. The snow coming down increased, and it turned into a truly mesmerizing experience. I felt as if we were inside a snow globe after it had been shaken up! I was savoring the huge rocking-chair sensation on his slow, extremely collected canter as the snow continued to swirl around us. I was so overwhelmed at the ultimate sensory sensations that I couldn't help but laugh out loud. We continued cantering around, and I leaned my head back with my face toward the sky, mouth open to catch snowflakes on my tongue. Lars seemed to be having just as much fun as I was, cantering around in a huge circle. I could see the flakes landing on his eyelashes. Time stood still, and that moment felt like it was lasting forever. Finally, Lars came back to a walk. I had him stop, and we just stood there as the snow kept falling. I leaned down and threw my arms around his warm neck to thank him for one of the most memorable experiences of my life. He turned his head and looked up at me, nodding his head up and down as if he truly understood.

CHAPTER 5

To this day, I can still see this all in my mind, and feel those sensations all over again. I see it as if I were watching myself in a movie, and also from the perspective of myself actually doing it.

VISUALIZING THROUGH THE DARKNESS

Life is many different things. It's beautiful, spontaneous, tragic, confusing, heartbreaking, and amazing. Most people experience all of these things at some point in their lives. Yes, life sometimes feels like a rollercoaster ride with its ups and downs. Of course, when it's good, you are happy and enjoying yourself. But what about the times when it is tragic, confusing, and heartbreaking? How do you get through it all?

My mom was my best friend. She was my only friend until I discovered I'm on the autism spectrum. This is common to those on the autism spectrum, to not have any friends and to be extremely close to one of their parents, or possibly both. In my case, it was my mom. She understood me and accepted me. As we later figured out, my mom was on the spectrum, too. That's why she understood me and accepted me! We were two peas in a pod. My dad never accepted that I'm different, and we weren't anywhere near as close as I was with my mom. They both lived with me, and I took care of both of them until they died.

Life as a certified registered nurse anesthetist is a busy one. Surgery starts early, around six thirty in the morning. On weekdays I have to get up at three o'clock to be at work by five. I then work the next nine hours at a high-stress job before coming home and taking care of both parents, my animals, cooking, cleaning, keeping up with bills, and tending to other aspects of everyday life. Physically, this was draining, but emotionally, it was devastating. Watching my mom's health decline, and my dad's Alzheimer's progress was, at times, totally consuming. Alzheimer's is a gradual disease. In the beginning it's not too bad, but then when it gets to the final stages it can be shocking. My mom had final stages of congestive heart failure and COPD. I was dealing with two totally different extremes. My dad's mental status was deteriorating rapidly. My mom, on the other hand, was sharp as a tack and had all her faculties, yet had a failing body.

I had to leave work early at times to take them to doctors' appointments: tests, MRIs, and other health-related things. My mom was using home oxygen at that point. I'd have to get her out to my truck in the wheelchair, the oxygen tank following in a little stand with wheels. It was tricky to get her out of the chair and into the vehicle without knocking over the oxygen tank or letting her fall. There were times I'd burst out crying in despair of the whole situation. Watching her gasp for air from the movement of getting up and into the truck was unbearable. By the time we got back home I was wiped out, yet had to keep going. I'd get her back into the house, get her food and water, then go take care of my dad. On days I had to take him to an appointment, it was like dealing with a two-year-old having a temper tantrum. He'd start by refusing to go anywhere. It took a lot of talking to finally get him ready to go, then out the door. At the office, there was the embarrassment of things he would say or do, common to end-stage Alzheimer's. That, too, was exhausting.

My only moments of reprieve were those when I went outside to stop and watch the sunset or look up at the stars. It was consuming to have all of this happening at one time. I can remember reading stories of people who took care of a parent until they died. I had two parents going at the same time. For many on the autism

CHAPTER 5

spectrum, it is enough to just care for themselves, let alone work full time and take care of two dying parents. Of course, it was constantly gnawing at the back of my mind that my mom was nearing the end. That was something I couldn't bear the thought of, yet I knew I had to. I turned to visualization. I forced myself to visualize that she was already gone, and how was I going to handle it. It was extremely difficult to visualize that. I would instantly become consumed with grief and hysteria inside, but I continued to force myself to do this. I don't know how others would deal with such a situation, but for me, that's what I had to do. My mom was my best friend, my confidant, my emotional support system, and the one who got me through other rough times.

It was about a week before she died when she talked me into calling hospice to come to the house. Mom recognized I was teetering on the edge of a physical and emotional collapse. I called the local hospice office and within two hours several people were at the house. They took over, quickly ordering a hospital bed for mom, placing an emergency kit into the refrigerator. They explained I was not to open that kit unless instructed by them over the phone to do so. It contained emergency drugs including morphine, which is a narcotic, and a controlled substance. The kit was sealed in shrink wrap, so they would know if it was tinkered with. They had other things brought to the house to assist in mom's care and they had the hospice grief counselor call me, as well. It all happened very fast. To say I was overwhelmed is an understatement. I'm sure even for neurotypicals it is overwhelming for all these people to come and start preparing for the inevitable. After they left the house, I flopped down on the couch and cried and cried. Mom was asleep as all that exhausted her as well. I kept visualizing ahead as to how I was going to handle it.

BECOMING AN AUTISM SUCCESS STORY

Several hours later, the hospice bed was delivered. It was brought in and set it up in the living room. After they left, my mom and I discussed just how were we going to get her up out of the recliner, into the wheelchair, and then onto the bed. Before we even attempted that, she wanted to talk. Even with the nasal cannula on providing oxygen, she was so out of breath. Yet she was determined to give me "instructions" on how to handle it once she was gone. It is extremely painful to write this, as I'm reliving those moments all over again. One bad thing about seeing in pictures is that when you think of things from the past, it is as if it is happening right now. Every last detail. I can see my mom as if she is here right now, hear her words, watch her gasp for air. Yes, it's grand for happy things, but it isn't happy to see all of that all over again.

There we sat for the next several hours, as she went over things she wanted me to do. There were two main issues she wanted to talk about. The first was how I was going to handle it when she died. Even in the end she was giving me support for the biggest thing I'd ever have to go through, losing her. I can still see myself crying and crying as she went on for hours telling me I'd be okay, and that I was well prepared to care for myself. I knew all her words were true, but it still wasn't going to make me feel better. For her second wish, she made me promise her that I was going to continue my work toward being an autism activist and helping others on the spectrum. She pointed out that at least I had her for fifty-three years in my life, always there for me and guiding me to do the right things. Many others didn't have anyone in their life, or they lost that one special person much earlier. She saw that I had much wisdom to offer others, so she wanted to be sure I didn't throw in the towel after she was gone. She said she knew it was going to be difficult for me, but in time I'd be doing much better. For some strange reason, she

CHAPTER 5

commented that five years from then, I'd be really happy and doing very well. At that time I couldn't see that to be the case, as I couldn't accept my life without her.

Several days later she left me, on August 9, 2013. The only reason I was able to function at that point was because I had visualized it ahead of time. As hysterical as I felt inside, I had to pick up the phone and call hospice. Two of them arrived in about twenty minutes. I gave them the name and number to the funeral home where she would get cremated and they handled that. For some reason, I called an acquaintance I knew to tell her what was happening. I occasionally met her and her husband for dinner. They had a son with autism, and that was our common ground. She happened to be home and said she was going to come over. She had met my mom one time a year earlier. She brought her son and told him to stay in another room while she talked to me. She stayed until the men came from the funeral home to get mom. Sometimes, something happens that makes a moment very surreal. The little boy was using his mom's phone to play songs online. Right as the workers had got my mom on the stretcher, the song "Music Box Dancer" began to play on the phone. I froze in my tracks. Many years ago, when I was in my early twenties, I was into ice dancing. Mom used to drive me to the ice-skating arena, and she also skated with me often. That was her favorite song and it was often played when we skated. All those memories flashed into my mind and I could feel us skating and see the vapor coming from our mouths in the cold arena. I couldn't even speak. How could this be? There are literally millions of songs, and this is the one that played in that moment. Then I remembered my mom's words just days earlier: she told me to remember the fifty-three years we had together and all the wonderful times. I think it was fate that her favorite song came right

153

then. It was one of the most profound moments of my life.

I didn't leave the house for the next month. Except for my husband, I have never shared the following with anyone. I stayed in bed for that month, but not in my bed. I stayed in that hospital bed that hospice brought, the bed Mom died in. I know it sounds ridiculous to some, but I needed to do that to feel close to her. That was where she took her last breath on this Earth. A week later, hospice called to make arrangements to come by and pick up the bed. I told them absolutely not. They inquired why I didn't want them to get the bed. I explained my reason, and then she said that wasn't a problem. She simply stated to call them when I was ready. I did have to get up to take care of my dad, but then I'd get right back in that bed. There I stayed, in the darkness, with my two cats and a dog snuggled all around me. They knew something was terribly wrong. Not one of them ever made a peep.

I would have starved to death if it had not been for my co-worker, the woman whose son was diagnosed with Asperger's. She had orchestrated with a few of our co-workers to bring food over each day. Some of them cooked really nice meals and others brought restaurant food. It was a very unexpected and very welcome surprise. They brought enough to feed my dad, as well. I was extremely grateful to them for their kindness.

As the days went on, I still couldn't get myself to return back to my bed. I began visualizing my life without my mom. How I was going to have to reshape my life? How I was going to function without her there for every step of the way? I had to rewire my brain as to how I was going to function without her. It was extremely difficult, but I obviously had no choice. One thing I had great difficulty with was rewiring my brain to not pick up the phone to call her. When we were apart, we would talk multiple times a day, even if it was just to say "hi, what's new?" It was kind of shocking when I went and picked up a phone to call her and it hit me like a ton of bricks that I could never do that again. If I hadn't used my visualization, I don't know how I would have ever gotten through what was honestly my darkest time. I had to visualize everything, as we did everything together. But now I was going to have to do everything alone.

It's five years to the day when my mom left this Earth. I still grieve for her every day. Not a day goes by that my heart doesn't feel those pangs of sorrow when I want to share a success with her, or wish I could ask her advice on something. I am not over my grief, and I never will be. The day I spoke at the United Nations, as I walked up the steps of that incredible building, I imagined what my mom would say if she could have seen me. I wished she could have seen me stand up in front of hundreds of people at a Future Horizons conference, sharing my entire life with them, and walking down the aisle and getting married to Abraham. All those moments that I want to share with her seem a bit less thrilling than if she were there to see it. Her face always lit up like a Christmas tree at the zany things I did, the exciting things I did, or the accomplishments I achieved. Yes, now I have Abraham. We are soul mates and best friends, as close as two human beings can possibly be. He knows, and accepts, those moments when I'm missing my mother with all my heart and just want her to see what I'm doing. He'll wrap his arms around me, hold me tightly, and cry with me. He never got to meet my mom, but I talk about her so much he feels as if he's known her his entire life. Abraham is grateful to her as well, because he has received all the wisdom from me that she gave me throughout my lifetime.

Then my brother died on February 12, 2014, six months after Mom. He had been battling esophageal cancer for years and had actually been doing well. In fact, he came to visit us in May of 2013, three months before mom died. That was the day he took me out to lunch and told me he was proud of everything I was doing and all my autism advocacy work. Until that very day, we were pretty much estranged. That's a whole different book. But that day, he was different, far different than he'd ever been. I guess he knew he didn't have long to go and wanted to make amends. I was so overwhelmed, as I saw he really meant it. After a lifetime of our distance, that moment changed everything. He seemed at peace. Several months later when his wife called to tell me the news, I burst out crying, sobbing so much I fell to the ground. It rarely ever snows in Pensacola. The night before, it did.

For a fleeting moment, I almost wished he didn't reconcile with me. That would have made it a whole lot easier to cope with the news. I went to share this with my dad. His end stages of Alzheimer's left him nothing more than a shell at that point. When I told him Wayne died, he asked who Wayne was. "Your son," I replied. He said he didn't have a son. He was annoyed that I interrupted his TV show. On April 6, 2014, two months later, my father died. I had hospice at the house for him, as well. My whole family was now gone. I felt like an orphan. I realize it sounds silly to be feeling like an orphan at the age of fifty-three, but that's the best way I could describe how I felt.

Looking back, I see that the only way I got through that time in my life was by visualizing. I had to visualize the future, how I was going to handle everything, and now I can visualize the past to remember all our great times together. I can visualize my mom giving me advice for things, apply it to the current situation, and feel confident that I know what to do. Of course, I can visualize all I want, but nothing can ever replace her still being here. But I'm thankful I knew to visualize, for that gift she gave me all those years ago when I was six years old: to always remember the power of the mind. It was the greatest gift I ever received.

AN AUTISM BASEBALL GAME: LOVE AND MARRIAGE

(Adapted from an article written for The Mighty.*)* [XXVI]

The first thing I did after I found out that I was on the autism spectrum was to start an Asperger's support group in my community. At one of those meetings, a man with autism came in with his mother. He was extremely timid and obviously had zero confidence and low self-esteem. We became friends and remained so for the next year.

Around that time, I purchased a hutch for my new bunny, but it sat in the box for weeks because I'm not good with assembling things. My new friend, Abraham, volunteered to put it together for me. He and his mother picked up the hutch so he could work at it at his home. One night, they brought it back to me totally assembled.

After putting the hutch up, we decided to stand out in my front driveway to enjoy the cool night and view the full moon and stars. Abraham made the move to lean over and hug me. That is a moment neither of us shall ever forget. As our arms embraced each other, and we felt the warmth of each other's bodies, a spark was ignited in both our souls. We couldn't let go of each other. We became one, and neither of us could tell where one ended and the other began. The painting, *The Kiss*, by Austrian symbolist painter Gustov Klimt flashed into my mind.

The feeling was so intense, so delicious, so shocking. Neither of us had ever expected to find anyone with whom we could have a relationship, much less marry. It seemed like an impossible dream. Suddenly, a fire was lit within each of us. I thought it was nothing like what most neurotypicals experience, because it was a spiritual fire, one extremely deep. It was on a level much greater than what most people ever experience or can understand.

Having autism surely has its challenges, but they are not, by any means, limitations. They are simply challenges. They force us to work harder to overcome our sensory sensitivities. Yet, those same challenges offer us the luxury to experience things on this higher level. Specifically, the sensory "issues" that are part of autism can also work positively for us.

Most people are familiar with the terms "getting to first base, second base, third base, or scoring a home run." First base is a kiss, while scoring a home run is actually having sex with someone. Second and third base are assigned to other degrees of intimacy! The baseball terms might work well for the neurotypical world, but I have a very different view, because relationships with others for those of us on the spectrum are not so easily gained, least of all intimate ones. We treasure the relationships that we do make and approach them from a very different perspective. Until that time of our hug, I never even had a friend. If a fleeting thought of finding a mate to have a relationship with or marry would surface in my head, I had always quickly dismissed that notion. How was that possible, when no one understood me except my mother? After being diagnosed with Asperger's, my entire life changed, primarily because I realized I was not the only person on Earth like me. I began meeting others on the spectrum, as well as people who wanted to work with us, because they wanted to be around us. But intimacy? It hadn't occurred to me. I had been too "different" my whole life.

So, that first hug far surpassed getting to first base, which neurotypicals boast about. We had both spent our lives "striking out" at simple relationships, much less emotionally charged ones. Neither one of us ever had friends; yet now, we realized the magical chemistry that drew us together. Hitting one out of the park is every batter's dream in a real baseball game. Abraham and I truly hit one out of the park with that hug.

Abraham proposed on Christmas Eve in 2014 underneath a towering blue spruce and a moonlit sky. The air was crisp and fresh, and he got down on one knee, just like in the movies. We already knew we were soul mates and couldn't stand being apart for a minute. We decided to marry on September 26, 2015 at the Love and Autism Conference. Dr. Tony Attwood, the world-renowned expert on the autism spectrum, commented on why he felt our wedding was important to the autism community.

He said,

My thoughts are that this is a special occasion that I want to be witnessed and experienced by those who truly appreciate the exchange of vows, as well as the importance of the union between two people from the same community.

Neurotypicals are notorious for not taking their wedding vows seriously. Those in the autism community take such vows very seriously and, from my experience, are very determined for the relationship to succeed and flourish. An autism-autism union is a very special occasion and an opportunity to celebrate the values, determination, and understanding of those within the same mindset who deeply love and value each other.

Congratulations on finding each other and finding love within and between each other.

Dr. Attwood's words so deeply touched my heart, because they are so very true. In today's society, people get married for many different reasons. Love isn't always one of them. People marry for financial gain, for moving up the social ladder, for prestige, political power, or just because it's expected.

A while back, Abraham and I attended our first baseball game together, a semi-pro game at our home-town stadium. We decided to go all out, and, upon arrival to the stadium, we headed into the team's merchandise store. There, we purchased baseball hats, flags to wave, and beads to hang around our necks.

As we emerged from the store, we now looked like the other five thousand people at the stadium. The music

CHAPTER 5

was loud but made us feel energetic. It was massive sensory overload, yet we were having a blast!

The next stop was one of the food establishments on the main concourse. We both ordered cheeseburgers and fries, a plastic baseball hat filled with popcorn, a big soft pretzel, and drinks. Trying to maintain our new hats, despite the Gulf breeze blowing, we made our way over to a ledge with our hands laden with all the food. There we stood, among the huge crowd, eating, cheering, and simply forgetting our autism, to have a hilarious, marvelous, astonishing time! We even took selfies to create memories of our night at the game. Our home team won, and we joined right in with the deafening roar of the crowd cheering them on and celebrating the win.

After the game, we drove down the street to the pier to admire the full moon, enjoy the ocean mist on our faces, and savor the sound of waves lapping against the pilings.

Our autism baseball game has been quite different than everyone else's.

LIFE COACHING

Over the past several years, I've had many different people from different walks of life ask me if I offer life coaching. Individuals on the autism spectrum, parents of individuals on the autism spectrum, neurotypicals, couples, and businessmen and women alike have all approached me on this topic. I have gained tremendous wisdom and life experiences, plus I have my keen sense of visualization, acceptance, inclusion, and an innate ability to follow my gut instinct; I realized I truly could help others by becoming a life coach. I am helping others already by being an autism activist, but this a different type of help.

I spent weeks researching and quickly discovered that there is a governing body which regulates those who coach, the International Coaching Federation. They are the gold standard of executive/life coaches. I found their list of institutions, researched all of them, and selected one of the top programs: The Rayner Institute in Calgary, Alberta. They offered many different levels of coaching, and I registered for the executive/life coaching program. It was a ten-week intensive training, twice a week for three hours. It was done online over video chat, which allowed the class and instructor to interact face-to-face. This program prepared me to serve as a life coach to individuals, and as an executive coaching to corporations for their employees. Upon completing the course, there was an exam and a requirement of 100 hours actual coaching time in order to apply for certification. Continuing education courses are required every two years to maintain your coaching certification.

I am very excited to begin my new journey as an executive/life coach! It is very rewarding to me to enable others to live their best lives possible. I am able to help them visualize what they want to do, be, or have, and figure out what they need to reach their dream.

CONCLUSION

"Far from being fixed, the brain is a highly dynamic structure, which undergoes significant change, not only as it develops, but also throughout the entire lifespan."
— *Moheb Costandi* [XXVII]

CHAPTER 5

Visualization should be the wave of the future in autism. Every parent worries what will become of their child with autism. This could be their answer. It's not just for those on the autism spectrum, because visualization is for anyone who wants to have a better life; but it is particularly relevant to those on the autism spectrum, who have the attributes of attention to detail, a desire for acceptance and understanding, visual thinking, and the ability to capture sensory experiences because they live with them daily on a hyper-level. Those should be viewed as attributes, not detriments. A young child or an older adult can change his life through visualization, whether for the person with autism or as a neurotypical.

As you come to the last page, I don't want you to see this as the end of the book. Instead, look at it as the beginning of your new life that awaits you! Always remember, you have within you the power of your mind. It is up to you to unleash this power and use it to reach your goals that you never thought possible. Share your success story with me at *anitalesko1@gmail.com* or through my website, *www.anitalesko.com*.

TAKE MY THIRTY-DAY CHALLENGE!

Here's what I'm going to ask you to do. Think of whatever your goal is that you'd like to achieve. Start out simple for your first time. Commit yourself to using my Seven Step Visualization strategy to rewire your brain through neuroplasticity for thirty days. Over that period of time, visualization will become second nature to you, enabling you to start utilizing it for many different things in your life.

REFERENCES

I.   Onderko, K. "What is Neuroplasticity?" Integrated Listening Systems, accessed January 2019, https://integratedlistening.com/what-is-neuroplasticity/?

II.   Warber, A. "Can the Autistic Brain Heal?" Love to Know, accessed January 2019, https://autism.lovetoknow.com/Can_the_Autistic_Brain_Heal

III.   Adams, T. "Norman Doidge: the man teaching us to change our minds," The Guardian, February 2015, https://www.theguardian.com/science/2015/feb/08/norman-doidge-brain-healing-neuroplasticity-interview

IV.   "Human-Animal Bond," American Veterinary Medical Association, accessed January 2019, https://www.avma.org/KB/Resources/Reference/human-animal-bond/Pages/Human-Animal-Bond-AVMA.aspx

V.   Angier N. "The Creature Connection," The New York Times, March 14, 2011, https://nytimes.com/2011/03/15/science/15why.html

VI.   "Autism Spectrum Disorder (ASD) Data & Statistics," Centers for Disease Control and Prevention, updated November 15, 2018, https://www.cdc.gov/ncbddd/autism/new-data.html

VII.   Williams A., "8 Successful People Who Use the Power of Visualization," Mind Body Green, accessed January 2019, https://www.mindbodygreen.com/0-20630/8-successful-people-who-use-the-power-of-visualization.html

VIII. Tellington-Jones, L. The Ultimate Horse Behavior and Training Book. Pomfret: Trafalgar Square Books, 2006.

IX.   "The Brain's Way of Healing," Norman Doidge MD website, accessed January 2019, http://www.normandoidge.com/?page_id=1042

X.   Aubele T. "Plastic is Fantastic…for Your Brain," Psychology Today, August 5, 2011, www.psychologytoday.com/us/blog/prime-your-gray-cells/201108/plastic-is-fantastic-your-brain

XI.   Niles, F. "How to Use Visualization to Achieve Your Goals," Huffington Post, updated August 17, 2011, https://www.huffpost.com/entry/visualization-goals_b_878424

XII.   Costandi, M. *Neuroplasticity: The MIT Press Essential Knowledge Series*. Massachusetts: The MIT Press, 2016.

XIII. "Hippotherapy," Equestrian Therapy, Horse Therapy for Special Needs, accessed January 2019, http://www.equestriantherapy.com/hippotherapy/

XIV.   "Therapeutic Horseback Riding," Therapeutic Equestrian Center, The Power of Horses, accessed January 2019, www.equestriantherapy.org/therapeutic-horseback-riding/

XV.   Nilson, R. "Equine-facilitated psychotherapy." *Perspectives in Psychiatric Care* (2004): 40(2), 42

XVI.   "The Temple Grandin Equine Center," Colorado State University College of Agricultural Sciences, accessed January 2019, https://tgec.agsci.colostate.edu/

XVII. Metzger M., "Temple Grandin Equine Center Groundbreaking Slated for 2018," *The Fence Post*, December 7, 2017, www.thefencepost.com/temple-grandin-equine-center-groundbreaking-slated-for-2018

REFERENCES

XVIII. Lasko, P. "The Positive Effects of Dressage on Children with Autism," *Dressage Today*, November 20, 2015, www.dressagetoday.com/lifestyle/the-positive-effects-of-dressage-on-children-with-autism-30479

XIX. "Horse Boy Foundation's Story," Horse Boy Foundation, accessed January 2019, https://www.horseboyfoundation.org/about

XX. "New Trails Learning Systems," New Trails Learning Systems, accessed January 2019, www.ntls.co

XXI. Grandin, T. "The use of therapy animals with individuals with autism spectrum disorders." *Science Direct* (2010). https://doi.org/10.1016/B978-0-12-381453-1.10013-3

XXII. Bayless, K. "What Is Helicopter Parenting?" Parents, accessed January 2019, https://www.parents.com/parenting/better-parenting/what-is-helicopter-parenting/

XXIII. Lesko, A. "How Childhood Jobs Prepared Me for Success as an Autistic Adult," The Mighty, September 15, 2016, https://themighty.com/2016/09/how-childhood-jobs-prepared-me-for-success-as-an-autistic-adult/

XXIV. Understood Contributors, "Understanding Executive Functioning Issues," Understood, accessed January 2019, https://understood.org/en/learning-attention-issues/child-learning-disabilities/executive-functioning-issues/understanding-executive-functioning-issues

XXV. Wikipedia contributors, "McDonnell Douglas F-15 Eagle," Wikipedia, The Free Encyclopedia, https://en.wikipedia.org/w/index.php?title=McDonnell_Douglas_F-15_Eagle&oldid=878505235(accessed January 18, 2019).

XXVI. Lesko, A. "What 'Getting to First Base' Meant for Us as a Couple on the Autism Spectrum," The Mighty, October 28, 2016, https://themighty.com/2016/10/getting-to-first-base-as-an-autistic-couple/

XXVII. Costandi, M. *Neuroplasticity: The MIT Press Essential Knowledge Series*. Massachusetts: The MIT Press, 2016.

ANITA LESKO, author of *Temple Grandin: The Stories I Tell My Friends*, is an internationally recognized autism advocate and member of Autism Society of America's Panel of Autistic Advisors. She was diagnosed with Asperger's syndrome at the age of fifty. A graduate of Columbia University, Anita was an honored speaker at the United Nations Headquarters for World Autism Awareness Day 2017. She is a contributing author for numerous publications including the *Autism Asperger's Digest* and *The Mighty*, and is a blogger for the International Board of Credentialing and Continuing Education Standards. Anita's first book, *Asperger's Syndrome: When Life Hands You Lemons, Make Lemonade*, a memoir, was written after she was diagnosed. She co-wrote *Been There. Done That. Try This! The Aspie's Guide to Life on Earth* with Dr. Tony Attwood and Craig Evans. She lives in Florida.